Vegan Instant Pot Cookbook

100 Amazingly Delicious Plant-Based Recipes for Fast, Easy, and Super Healthy Vegan Pressure Cooker Meals

Vanessa Olsen

ISBN: 1541273885
ISBN-13: 978-1541273887

Table of Contents

Introduction

A healthy diet is key to having a happy, fulfilling life. A diet too full of unhealthy foods results in fatigue and vulnerability to diseases, many of them serious. Unfortunately, our society is not lacking in unhealthy options. To meet demand, companies turn to unethical methods, resulting in animal cruelty. Health and the treatment of animals are two of the main reasons why people commit to veganism, a plant-based diet that also eliminates animal products like milk, cheese, gelatin, and honey.

Getting the most nutrition out of every food is very important for vegans, and that's where pressure cooking shines. Pressure cookers are able to retain the most nutrition possible from vegetables and beans, and the appliance makes healthy cooking extremely easy. While there are packaged vegan options, making your own meals is always the healthy alternative, and much less expensive. This book presents the first steps in becoming a vegan, and provides 100 recipes for breakfasts, entrees, sides, desserts, and more, so you have a strong foundation to build off of.

Whether you're already a vegan and just need more recipe options, or have just started considering transitioning your diet, this book will give you everything you need to succeed

VANESSA OLSEN

Chapter 1

What's Vegan Cooking All About?

Veganism has become very popular in recent times, as people realize just how unhealthy society's eating habits have become. We are a meat-loving culture, and sadly, go to unethical lengths to get the meat we crave. Because of health concerns, ethical concerns, or both, more people are deciding to give up meat and, differing from vegetarians, *all* animal products. Their diet shifts to one based on whole grains, vegetables, fruit, beans, nuts, seeds, and vegan versions of popular foods.

When did veganism start?

Evidence for veganism has existed for 2,000 years, but the movement didn't have an official platform until the 1940's. Donald Watson, an English vegetarian who did not consume dairy, met with five others who shared his vision to talk through ways to spread

3

their message. They disliked the label "non-dairy vegetarians," because it was clunky, and ended up deciding on "vegans." The Vegan Society was born. Watson is considered the father of modern veganism, and until his death at age 95, he advocated for organic farming and pacifism.

What are the benefits of veganism?

A diet free from all animal products has a lot of benefits. Just a handful include:

- More energy
- Healthier skin, hair, and nails
- Fewer migraines
- Fewer colds and flus
- Improved heart health
- Improved resistance to cancer

While studies have shown that veganism can lead to a lower BMI, it should not be adopted purely for the sake of weight loss. "Vegan" does not mean "lower-calorie," and other healthy habits like exercise and drinking water should accompany the diet if you want to lose weight.

Chapter 2

How to Transition to a Vegan Diet

Wanting to become a vegan? How would you go about it? There are really only two steps when you break it down: adding food, and then cutting out food and replacing it.

When you're starting out on your vegan journey, the easiest first step is to start adding food into your diet rather than cutting it out. That means buying more fruits, vegetables, whole grains, beans, tofu, nuts, and so on. You start making vegan recipes alongside non-vegan ones, and familiarizing yourself with vegan brands. This way, you can see just how many options you do have, and figuring out what you do and don't like, without feeling like you're starving.

Once you've been adding vegan food to your diet for a little while, it's time to start cutting out food. The good thing about this step is you don't have to say goodbye to them entirely. What you do is cut out, and then replace. That means instead of drinking milk, you start getting dairy alternatives like soy, almond, or even cashew milk. Instead of regular cheese, find a vegan cheese brand.

The art of substitution is key to being a vegan with a varied diet. Here are some classic subs that vegans rely on:

- ## Eggs

  For cooking, crumbled tofu is very similar in texture to scrambled eggs. For baking, subs include applesauce, flax eggs, and mashed bananas. As a binder, oat and soy flour, rolled oats, bread crumbs, potato flakes, and cornstarch work well.

- ## Beef/chicken stock

  Veggie stock is the obvious alternative, and many vegan food brands make stocks that taste like chicken or beef.

- ## Butter

  Vegetable oils and vegan margarines (like Earth Balance) are popular.

- ## Yogurt

  There are soy and coconut oil yogurts with different flavors that can be eaten straight or used in baking.

- ## Gelatin

  Used in baking, gelatin can be replaced with agar powder or agar flakes.

Stocking a vegan pantry

What does a vegan's pantry and fridge look like? When you go to the store, what should you stock up on? Here is a sample list you can use as a reference, so if you ever feel like you're running out of options, take a look back and see how varied a vegan diet can really be.

- Canned/dry beans (especially lentils and chickpeas)
- Whole grains/flours (quinoa, brown rice, white rice, almond flour, all-purpose flour, rolled oatmeal, steel-cut oats, seitan)
- Nuts (walnuts, cashews, almonds, pine nuts)
- Dried fruit (dates, dried cranberries, prunes, raisins)
- Fresh fruit (whatever is in season, bananas, apples, lemons)
- Fresh vegetables (whatever is in season)
- Canned/frozen vegetables (tomatoes, corn, carrots, peas, green beans)
- Non-dairy milks (almond milk, soy milk)
- Pickled vegetables (jalapenos, pickles
- Tofu/Tempeh
- Bread
- Apple cider vinegar
- Cornstarch
- Vegetable broth
- Nutritional yeast
- Miso/Tahini
- Maple syrup
- Agave syrup
- Sugar
- Coconut oil
- Olive oil
- Ground flax seeds

- Dark chocolate
- Nut butters
- Salsa
- Tortilla chips
- Balsamic vinegar
- Dried herbs and seasonings

A lot of vegans like to be oil-free if possible, so there are a bunch of recipes in this book that do not contain coconut oil, olive oil, and so on.

These are clearly marked **(Oil Free)**, so you can quickly see in the Table of Contents what recipes are available.

Chapter 3

The Instant Pot Is a Vegan's Dream

A vegan really cannot do without an Instant Pot pressure cooker. Time and time again, pressure cookers have been proven to be the best way to cook food when nutritional value is the highest priority. This is because pressure cookers are so fast, and the faster something cooks, the more nutrition is retained. Fruits, veggies, beans, and whole grains - the types of food that a vegan lives off - keep nearly 100% of their nutrients.

Why the Instant Pot? It's the most popular electric pressure cooker brand available now, and very reasonably priced. Vegan food bloggers rave about it. There are a few variations of the Instant Pot, but in order to make all the recipes in this book, the 7-in-1 is recommended because it has the Yogurt program and you can adjust to high or low pressure.

Using the Instant Pot

The Instant Pot is not hard to figure out. It consists of three parts: the lid, the inner pot, and the base. The lid is the most important part of the cooker, because it is designed to provide the airtight seal that allows pressure to build and the boiling point of water to go up. The lid has a steam release handle, which needs to be in the "sealing" position when you're cooking. When the recipe is complete and it calls for a "quick-release" or "manual release," you turn the handle to "venting." If the recipe calls for a "natural release," it means you turn off the cooker and wait for the pressure to come down on its own. Want to know if the pressure is all gone? Look at the float valve, which is a little pin on the lid that is either up or down. Up means there's still pressure, while down means you can open the pot.

The inner pot of the pressure cooker is where the food actually cooks. It's basically just like your other pots, nothing too special or technological about it.

The base is the cooker's brain. The control panel is where you set all your pressures and times and what not. It looks intimidating, but it's pretty self-explanatory:

- **Sauté**: You'll be using this setting a lot in this book. You use it whenever you need to cook aromatics (onions, garlic, herbs, etc.) or brown something. This is a non-pressurized setting, which means you keep the lid off.

- **Keep Warm/Cancel**: Another setting you'll get to know well. Hitting "cancel" will turn off your pressure cooker or reset it, if you hit the wrong button. You can also use this setting to keep the food in your cooker warm until you're ready to serve.

- **Manual:** You pretty much use this button every time in the recipes. When you hit this, you then choose the pressure you want and length of time you'll be cooking.

- **The "-" and "+" buttons:** You hit one of these two buttons after hitting "manual," so you can adjust to the proper cooking time. You can also select these buttons after choosing a specific program, because there are default times on those, and you don't necessarily want to use them.

- **Pressure:** After choosing your cooking time, you can hit this button to specify what pressure you want to use.

- **Soup:** This program sets the cooker for high pressure for 30 minutes.

- **Meat/Stew:** This program sets the cooker for preparing meats for high pressure for 35 minutes. You won't have to worry about this one.

- **Poultry:** Sets the cooker for chicken, turkey, etc. on high pressure for 15 minutes.

- **Beans/Chili:** Sets the cooker for beans and chili on high pressure for 30 minutes.

- **Rice:** Sets cooker on low pressure. The Instant Pot selects its own cooking time depending on the amount of rice and water you have in the Pot.

- **Multi-grain:** Sets the cooker for grains on high pressure for 40 minutes.

- **Porridge:** Sets the cooker for porridge on high pressure for 20 minutes.

- **Steam:** Sets the cooker for 10 minutes on high pressure.

- **Yogurt:** Used only for starting a yogurt cycle on the Instant Pot.

- **<u>Slow Cook:</u>** Sets cooker to operate like a slow cooker.

Even with all those programs, we will really only use **four** in these recipes: "Sauté," "Manual," "Keep Warm/Cancel," and the "-" and "+" buttons. You don't even have to worry about setting the pressure unless the recipe calls for low pressure, because the cooker automatically assumes you'll be using high pressure when you hit "manual."

When you make a recipe, you'll notice references to a steamer basket or trivet. These are essentials for any pressure cooker, because a lot of food should not directly touch the bottom of the cooker while cooking, or it will burn. Steamer baskets and trivets perform the same function, so it really doesn't matter which you use, if you don't want to get both.

The next chapter will go over how to clean your pressure cooker, so you can keep using it for years to come.

.

Chapter 4

Maintaining the Instant Pot

Like any piece of kitchen equipment, you should take good care of your Instant Pot if you want to make the most of it. Luckily, cleaning the pot is pretty easy. The outside can get dusty and grimy with food stuff, so just wipe down with a paper towel and spray solution. To avoid lingering odors, keep the lid off the cooker when not in use.

The main part you'll have to clean is the actual inner pot, where the food goes. You wash this like you would any saucepan, and if you want, you can put it in the dishwasher. If you wash by hand right away, however, you can use the pot again right away, and food doesn't harden. Plain ol' soap and hot water is all that's needed, and a soft sponge, as anything abrasive will scratch the stainless steel.

The lid should also be cleaned, and there are two specific parts on it that can be tricky, so I have attached a picture for you to look at. There is a metallic "plug" on the inside of the lid that foamy foods can get into. This is the anti-block shield, and it does come off the lid. Don't twist it, just pull. It may seem like it's not going to come off, so be careful and pull hard. Clean the inside of the guard, and with a knitting needle (or something else made of metal and thin enough to fit in the hole), just poke inside the tiny valve.

13

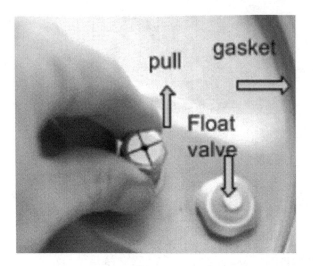

The second part of the lid that should be washed is the silicone ring or, more officially, the gasket. Just rub it with some soap and warm water. If it starts to smell or stain, soak for at least 15 minutes. Gaskets wear out over time, so eventually you have to buy a new one. The last part of the lid that can be cleaned is the float valve. It has a tiny silicone ring on it that can absorb smells and residue, so just pop it off, wipe clean, dry, and fit it back on.

Chapter 5

Essential Cooking Charts

There are a lot of ingredients you'll be working with in the recipes, and there will be times when you want to just cook a single ingredient, like rice or broccoli. As a handy reference, look to these charts to see how long you should cook it and what pressure to use.

Grains	Electric cooker	Stovetop cooker	Pressure
Oats (steel-cut)	3	3	High
Oats (rolled)	10	10	High
Brown rice	20	18	High

15

Jasmine rice (rinsed)	1	1	Low or high
White (long-grain) rice	3	3	Low or high
Amaranth	8	8	High
Barley flakes	20	18	High
Pearl barley	20	18	High
Buckwheat	2	2	High
Millet	1	1	High
Quinoa	1	1	High

Fruit	Electric cooker	Stovetop cooker	Pressure
Apples	3	2	High
Blackberries	6	6	High
Cherries	2	2	High
Chestnuts (fresh)	8	5	High
Figs (fresh)	3	4	Low/High

Figs (dried)	8	6	Low/High
Peaches (whole/fresh)	4	2	High
Pears (dried)	5	4	High
Pears (fresh, halved)	4	3	Low
Prunes	5	4	High
Raisins	5	4	High

Vegetables	Electric cooker	Stovetop cooker	Pressure
Cabbage	3	3	Low/High
Collards	1	1	Low/High
Eggplant	2-3	2-3	Low/High
Green beans (fresh/frozen)	2-3	2-3	Low/High
Kale	1	1	Low/High
Mushrooms (dry)	10	8	Low/High

Mushrooms (fresh)	5	5	Low/High
Artichoke hearts	3	3	Low or high
Broccoli	3 to 5	3 to 5	Low or high
Carrots (sliced)	1 to 2	1 to 2	Low or high
Cauliflower (florets)	2 to 3	2 to 3	Low or high
Corn on the cob	5	5	Low or high
Onions	3	3	Low or high
Peas (fresh or frozen)	2 to 3	2 to 3	Low or high
Bell peppers	3 to 4	3 to 4	Low or high
Whole sweet potatoes	15	10	High
Butternut squash (halves)	6	6	Low or high
Beets (whole)	25	20	High

Beets (small, whole)	15	12	High
Black beans (soaked)	6	4	High
White beans (soaked)	8	6	High
Tomatoes (whole)	3	3	High
Tomatoes (quartered)	2	2	High
Brussels sprouts	4	3	High
Parsnips (½ inch slices)	4	2	High
Pumpkin (1-2 inch slices)	4	2	High
Acorn squash (halved)	8	6	High
Spaghetti squash (halved)	12	10	High
Onions	3	3	Low or high

Before we move on to the recipes, it's important to make a note about time. The cooking time for any given recipe can vary a lot depending on what altitude you live in. High altitudes mean a longer cooking time. Because of this, the cooking time listed in the recipes does *not* factor in the length of time it takes for the cooker to actually reach pressure, the time represents how long the cooker *stays* at pressure.

Chapter 6

Breakfast

Pear Oats with Walnuts

<u>Serves</u>: 4

<u>Time</u>: 6 minutes

Rolled oats are one of the fastest cooking foods with the Instant Pot. For this recipe, you mix everything in a bowl, which sets in the steamer rack in the pressure cooker. The oats cook in almond milk, sugar, and just a tablespoon of coconut oil. Fresh pears will soften beautifully in there, as well, and you finish it off with cinnamon and walnuts.

<u>Ingredients:</u>

2 cups almond milk
2 cups peeled and cut pears
1 cup rolled oats
½ cup chopped walnuts
¼ cup sugar
1 tablespoon melted coconut oil
¼ teaspoon salt
Dash of cinnamon

<u>Directions:</u>

1. Mix everything except the walnuts and cinnamon in an oven-safe bowl that you know fits in the Instant Pot.
2. Pour 1 cup of water into the pressure cooker and lower in steamer rack.
3. Put the bowl on top and lock the lid.
4. Select "manual," and then high pressure for 6 minutes.

5. When time is up, quick-release the pressure.
6. Carefully remove the bowl, divide into 4 servings, and season with salt and cinnamon.

Nutritional Info (¼ recipe):

Total calories: 288
Protein: 5
Carbs: 39
Fiber: 4.5
Fat: 13

Banana-Buckwheat Porridge (Oil Free)

Serves: 3-4
Time: 26 minutes (6 minutes cook time, 20 minutes natural release)

Buckwheat is a good oat-alternative if you're sensitive to gluten. It's also high in fiber and has comparable health benefits to fruits and veggies! Because of its texture, buckwheat takes a little longer to cook than rolled oats, so you need to do a natural pressure release to make sure it's soft enough.

Ingredients:

3 cups almond (or rice) milk
1 cup buckwheat groats
1 sliced banana
¼ cup raisins
1 teaspoon cinnamon
½ teaspoon pure vanilla extract

Directions:

1. Rinse off the buckwheat and put right in the Instant Pot.
2. Pour in the milk, and add the rest of the ingredients.
3. Lock the lid.
4. Select "manual," and then cook for 6 minutes on high pressure.
5. When time is up, hit "cancel" and wait 20 minutes or so for the pressure to go all the way down.
6. Open the lid and stir well. Add more milk if it's too thick for

24

you.
7. Serve!

Nutritional Info (¼ recipe):

Total calories: 240
Protein: 6
Carbs: 46
Fiber: 5
Fat: 4

Pumpkin Spice Oatmeal w/ Brown Sugar Topping (Oil Free)

Serves: 6-8
Time: 15 minutes (3 minutes cook time, 12 minutes natural release)

If someone tells you that vegan food is bland, serve them this breakfast and they'll change their mind. It uses steel-cut oats, pumpkin puree, cinnamon, and allspice. The brown sugar, chopped pecan topping is just as delicious and adds a nice crunch.

Cooking Tip: If you like really soft oats, cook for at least 7 minutes instead of 3.

Ingredients:

4 ½ cups water
1 ½ cups steel-cut oats
1 ½ cups pumpkin puree
2 teaspoons cinnamon
1 teaspoon vanilla
1 teaspoon allspice

½ cup brown sugar
¼ cup chopped pecans
1 tablespoon cinnamon

Directions:

1. Pour 1 cup water into the pressure cooker.

2. Add everything from the first ingredient list (including rest of the water) into an oven-safe bowl and set in the steamer basket.
3. Lower basket into the Instant Pot and lock the lid.
4. Select "manual," and cook on high pressure for 3 minutes.
5. When time is up, hit "cancel" and wait for the pressure to come down on its own.
6. Mix the topping ingredients in a small bowl.
7. When you serve, sprinkle on top. If necessary, add a little almond milk to the oats.

Nutritional Info (⅛ recipe):

Total calories: 207
Protein: 4
Carbs: 38
Fiber: 4
Fat: 4

Chai-Spiced Oatmeal with Mango (Oil Free)

<u>Serves</u>: 2-3

<u>Time</u>: 13 minutes (3 minutes cook time, 10 minutes natural release)

A fan of chai tea? This oatmeal mimics those spicy-sweet flavors with cinnamon, ginger, cloves, and cardamom. The measurements are in "dashes," because it's up to you how much of each spice you want, depending on your tastes. Top the bowl off with some fresh-cut mango, or whatever fruit you like.

Cooking Tip: Cardamom and cloves are really strong, so add a teeny amount and taste.

<u>Ingredients:</u>

3 cups water
1 cup steel-cut oats
½ teaspoon vanilla
Dash of cinnamon
Dash of ginger
Dash of cloves
Dash of cardamom
Dash of salt
½ mango, cut into pieces

<u>Directions:</u>
1. Mix water and oats in the Instant Pot.
2. Close the lid.
3. Select "manual," and cook for 3 minutes on high pressure.

4. When the beeper sounds, hit "cancel" and wait for the pressure to come down naturally.
5. Open the lid and stir well.
6. Season and taste.
7. Divide into even servings and add chopped mango.

Nutritional Info (⅓ recipe):

Total calories: 236
Protein: 6
Carbs: 44
Fiber: 5.5
Fat: 4

Coconut-Almond Risotto (Oil Free)

Serves: 4
Time: 20 minutes (10 minutes cook time, 10 minutes natural release)

Risotto is usually reserved for savory side dishes, but it's a perfect vehicle for sweeter breakfasts, too. Using vanilla almond milk and coconut milk adds flavor and a beautiful creaminess. For texture, a topping of coconut flakes and sliced almonds is perfect.

Ingredients:

2 cups vanilla almond milk
1 cup coconut milk
1 cup Arborio rice
⅓ cup sugar
2 teaspoons pure vanilla
¼ cup sliced almonds and coconut flakes

Directions:

1. Pour the milks into the Instant Pot and hit the "sauté" button.
2. Stir until it boils.
3. Add the rice and stir before locking the lid.
4. Select "manual," and cook for 5 minutes on high pressure.
5. When time is up, press "cancel" and wait 10 minutes. Quick-release any leftover pressure.
6. Add the sugar and vanilla.
7. Divide up oats and top with almonds and coconut.

Nutritional Info (¼ recipe):

Total calories: 337
Protein: 6
Carbs: 66
Fiber: 1.5
Fat: 7

Soy Yogurt (Oil Free)

Makes: 8 cups
Time: 12 hours to make + 6 hours in fridge before eating

Vegan yogurt? Yes, it's possible. It's a lot of waiting, but very little work. To make this recipe, you'll need the Instant Pot 7-in-1, which has the Yogurt program. To ensure this yogurt is vegan, make sure to get a soymilk that only lists water and soybeans in the ingredients.

Ingredients:

2 quarts of soy milk
1 packet of vegan yogurt culture

Directions:

1. Mix milk and yogurt culture together.
2. Pour into a heatproof container that you know fit in your Instant Pot. Leave off any lids.
3. Put into the Instant Pot. You do **not** need to add any water to the pot because it doesn't actually rise to pressure!
4. Close the lid and select the "yogurt" button. Adjust time to 12 hours for a professional-quality thick, creamy yogurt.
5. Go about your business until time is up, and then take out the yogurt.
6. Put the lids on the containers and store in the fridge for at least 6 hours.
7. The yogurt will be very tangy, so sweeten with vanilla, sugar, jam, fruit, and so on!

Nutritional Info (1 cup):

Total calories: 55
Protein: 4
Carbs: 5
Fiber: .5
Fat: 2

Banana-Amaranth Porridge (Oil Free)

Serves: 4
Time: 13 minutes (3 minutes cook time, 10 minutes natural release)

Amaranth is an ancient "grain," though it technically isn't a grain at all. It's basically a bud, but has similar health benefits to other cereals, and it makes a darn tasty hot porridge. This recipe uses no added sugar; bananas add the sweetness.

Ingredients:

2 ½ cups unsweetened almond milk
1 cup amaranth
2 sliced bananas
Dash of cinnamon

Directions:

1. Mix the amaranth, milk, and bananas in your Instant Pot.
2. Seal the lid.
3. Select "manual," and cook on high pressure for just 3 minutes.
4. When time is up, hit "cancel" and wait for the pressure to come down on its own.
5. When all the pressure is gone, you can serve the porridge with cinnamon.

Nutritional Info (¼ recipe):

Total calories: 271
Protein: 8
Carbs: 47
Fiber: 3.25
Fat: 6

Black Bean + Sweet Potato Hash (Oil Free)

<u>Serves</u>: 4
<u>Time</u>: About 15 minutes (5 minutes prep time, 10 minutes cook time)

Hashes make a great breakfast, because they're easy to make and easy to make nutritious. This one uses protein-heavy black beans and sweet potatoes. A little chili powder adds some heat to wake up even the sleepiest commuters.

<u>Ingredients</u>:

2 cups peeled, chopped sweet potatoes
1 cup chopped onion
1 cup cooked and drained black beans
1 minced garlic clove
⅓ cup veggie broth
¼ cup chopped scallions
2 teaspoons hot chili powder

<u>Directions</u>:

1. Prep your veggies.
2. Turn your Instant Pot to "sauté" and cook the chopped onion for 2-3 minutes, stirring so it doesn't burn.
3. Add the garlic and stir until fragrant.
4. Add the sweet potatoes and chili powder, and stir.
5. Pour in the broth and give one last stir before locking the lid.
6. Select "manual," and cook on high pressure for 3 minutes.
7. When time is up, quick-release the pressure carefully.

8. Add the black beans and scallions, and stir to heat everything up.
9. Season with salt and more chili powder if desired.

Nutritional Info (¼ recipe):

Total calories: 133
Protein: 5
Carbs: 28
Fiber: 9.5
Fat: 1

Cranberry-Walnut Quinoa (Oil Free)

Serves: 4
Time: 10 minutes

This breakfast bowl tastes like the holidays. You just cook up quinoa and mix in dried cranberries, chopped walnuts, and sunflower seeds. Add a favorite vegan sweetener and cinnamon.

Ingredients:

2 cups water
2 cups dried cranberries
1 cup quinoa
1 cup chopped walnuts
1 cup sunflower seeds
½ tablespoon cinnamon

Directions:

1. Rinse quinoa.
2. Put quinoa, water, and salt in the Instant Pot.
3. Lock the lid.
4. Select "manual," and cook for 10 minutes on high pressure.
5. When the timer beeps, hit "cancel" and quick-release.
6. When the pressure is gone, open the cooker.
7. Mix in the dried cranberries, nuts, seeds, sweetener, and cinnamon.
8. Serve and enjoy!

Nutritional Info (¼ recipe):

Total calories: 611
Protein: 13
Carbs: 85
Fiber: 5.25
Fat: 29

Breakfast Tofu Scramble (Oil Free)

Serves: 4
Time: 9 minutes (5 minutes prep time, 4 minutes cook time)

Breakfast scrambles are quick, easy, and you can add just about anything you want. This recipe includes cherry tomatoes, a potato, and an apple. Instead of eggs, you use crumbled tofu. Seasonings are up to you, as well, and since tofu is pretty bland, don't be shy.

Ingredients:

1 block of extra-firm, crumbled tofu
1 cup cherry tomatoes
1 onion
1 diced potato
1 diced apple
¼ cup veggie broth
2 minced garlic cloves
1 teaspoon dry dill
½ teaspoon ground turmeric
Salt and pepper to taste

Directions:

1. Turn your Instant pot to sauté and dry-cook the garlic and onion until the onion begins to soften.
2. Add a bit of water if it starts to stick.
3. Pour broth into cooker, and add the rest of the ingredients.
4. Select "manual" and cook on high pressure for 4 minutes.
5. When time is up, hit "cancel" and quick-release.

6. Stir, season to taste, and enjoy!

<u>Nutritional Info (¼ recipe)</u>:

Total calories: 139
Protein: 12
Carbs: 15
Fiber: 1
Fat: 5

CHAPTER 6 - BREAKFAST

Chapter 7

One-Pot Meals

Millet Bowl with Lentils and Sugar-Snap Peas (Oil Free)

<u>Serves</u>: 4
<u>Time</u>: 35 minutes (10 minutes prep time, 25 minutes cook time)

Millet is a tiny grain found in birdseed, but when you cook it in a pressure cooker, it expands into a nutty, fluffy dish similar to quinoa. Perfect for lunch or dinner, this bowl also includes sugar-snap peas, mushrooms, onions, and lentils.

<u>Ingredients:</u>

2 ¼ cups veggie stock
1 cup rinsed millet
1 cup sliced onion
1 cup sliced sugar snap peas
½ cup oyster mushrooms
½ cup rinsed green lentils
¼ cup chopped parsley
2 minced garlic cloves
Dash of lemon juice
Dash of salt

<u>Directions:</u>

1. Prep your ingredients.
2. Turn your Instant Pot to "sauté" and add garlic, onion, and mushrooms.
3. After 2 minutes, add the millet and lentils, and stir for 1 minute.
4. Pour in the stock.
5. Lock and seal the lid.
6. Select "manual," and then 10 minutes on high pressure.
7. When time is up, hit "cancel" and let the pressure come down on its own.

8. Pour in the peas and close the lid for a few minutes, without bringing to pressure, to heat everything through.
9. Stir and add the herbs.
10. Divide into bowls and squeeze some lemon juice on each serving.

Nutritional Info (¼ recipe):

Total calories: 230
Protein: 7
Carbs: 45
Fiber: 4.25
Fat: 2

Sweet Potato + Black-Eyed Pea Bowl

Serves: 4

Time: About 25 minutes (5 minutes prep time, 20 minutes cook time)

Sweet potatoes are hearty and a great vehicle for spices. For this bowl, the spices of choice include garlic, cumin, and coriander. For protein, you've got black-eyed peas, the Instant Pot cooks perfectly.

Ingredients:

3-4 halved sweet potatoes
1 ½ cups water
2 cups spinach
1 cup rinsed black-eyed peas
1 chopped onion
4 smashed garlic cloves
1 tablespoon olive oil
1 tablespoon tomato paste
1 teaspoon cumin seeds
½ teaspoon coriander seeds
Dash of salt

Directions:

1. Prep your ingredients.
2. Put the potatoes (cut-side up) in the steamer basket.
3. Hit "sauté" on your Instant Pot and add olive oil.
4. When hot, sauté onion.
5. When the onion is soft, add garlic and cool for a minute.
6. Add black-eyed peas, water, and tomato paste, and stir.
7. Lower in the steamer basket with potatoes.
8. Lock and seal the lid.
9. Select "manual," and cook for 12 minutes on high pressure.
10. When time is up, quick-release the pressure.

11. Take out the potatoes.
12. Add spinach to the Instant Pot and a dash of salt, and let the leaves wilt.
13. Serve, with two potato halves per guest!

Nutritional Info (¼ recipe):

Total calories: 273.6
Protein: 8.2
Carbs: 48.5
Fiber: 9.8
Fat: 6.3

Red Curry + Sweet Potato Bowl (Oil Free)

Serves: 4-6
Time: About 20 minutes (5 minutes prep time, 20 minutes natural release)

Are you hungry for a spicy, veggie-full bowl of goodness that will warm you on cool nights? This lentil-and-sweet potato bowl is flavored with Thai red curry paste, so you don't have to mess with a lot of expensive whole spices. That heat is mellowed out with coconut milk.

Ingredients:

1 pound peeled and cubed sweet potatoes
1 ¾ cups veggie stock
1 large chopped onion
4 minced garlic cloves
1 cup cauliflower florets
½ cup green lentils
½ cup coconut milk
1 tablespoon lime juice
2 teaspoons Thai red curry paste

Directions:

1. Prep your ingredients.
2. Turn your Instant Pot to "sauté" and cook the onion for about 1 minute.
3. Add garlic and cook for another minute.
4. Add ¾ cup veggie stock, lentils, curry paste, and coconut milk.
5. Close and seal the lid.
6. Choose "manual," and then cook for 3 minutes on high pressure.
7. When time is up, hit "cancel" and let the pressure come down by itself.
8. Add, cubed potato and 1 cup of stock.

9. Close the lid again and seal.
10. Select "manual" again, and cook for 10 minutes.
11. When the timer beeps, quick-release the pressure this time.
12. Add broccoli and close the lid to let the leftover heat cook the broccoli.
13. Season and serve!

Nutritional Info (¼ recipe):
Total calories: 201
Protein: 7
Carbs: 38
Fat: 5
Fiber: 5.5

Tofu, Kale, and Sweet Potato Bowl

Serves: 2-4
Time: Under 10 minutes (3 minutes cook time)

Tofu is the perfect vehicle for all sorts of flavors. It's like a taste sponge, and for this recipe, it's absorbing flavors from onion, fresh garlic, ginger, and cayenne pepper. Sweet potatoes and kale leaves add body, sweetness, and antioxidants.

Ingredients:

1 peeled and cut sweet potato
2 cups sliced kale leaves (stems and ribs removed)
8 ounces cubed tofu
1 chopped onion
2 minced garlic cloves
¼-½ cup veggie broth
1-3 teaspoons tamari
1 teaspoon ground ginger
½ teaspoon ground cayenne
1 teaspoon olive oil
Squeeze of lemon juice

Directions:

1. After prepping your ingredients, turn your Instant Pot to "sauté" and add oil.
2. When hot, sauté the tofu for a minute.
3. Mix in the tamari with a few tablespoons of broth.
4. Stir for a minute.
5. Add sweet potatoes, onion, garlic, and the rest of the broth.
6. Select "manual," and cook on high pressure for 2 minutes.
7. When time is up, hit "cancel" and quick-release.
8. Throw in the kale and seal back up for another 1 minute on high

pressure.
9. Quick-release.
10. Divide up the meal and serve with a squirt of fresh lemon.

Nutritional Info (¼ recipe):

Total calories: 133
Protein: 11
Carbs: 13
Fiber: 2.25
Fat: 5

Mexican Casserole (Oil Free)

<u>Serves</u>: 4
<u>Time</u>: 28 minutes (+ 2-hours soak time for beans)

Get ready to make the easiest casserole ever. You just need rice, beans, tomato paste, and a few spices. It's a great option for when you're trying to put off going to the store, but you don't want to eat a dinner of crackers and peanut butter.

<u>Ingredients:</u>

5 cups water
2 cups uncooked brown rice
1 cup soaked black beans
6-ounces tomato paste
2 teaspoons chili powder
2 teaspoons onion powder
1 teaspoon garlic
1 teaspoon salt

<u>Directions:</u>

1. A few hours before dinner, put your dry beans in a bowl with enough water to cover them.
2. Soak on the countertop for at least two hours and drain.
3. Put everything in your Instant Pot.
4. Close and seal the pressure cooker.
5. Select "manual," and then cook on high pressure for 28 minutes.
6. When time is up, hit "cancel" and quick-release.
7. Taste and season more if necessary.

Nutritional Info (¼ recipe):

Total calories: 322
Protein: 6
Carbs: 63
Fiber: 9
Fat: 2

Black-Eyed Pea Masala (Oil Free)

<u>Serves</u>: 8

<u>Time</u>: 1 hour, 30 minutes (1 hour for bean prep, 7 minutes cook time, 20 minutes natural release)

This classic Indian dish usually has a "chicken" before the "masala," but to veganize it, you use black-eyed peas instead. To cut down on time, you can quick-soak the beans by boiling them for 1 minute, and then letting them sit for at least 1 hour. Garam masala is a spice mix you can get just about anywhere.

<u>Ingredients:</u>

2 cups water
2 cups dried black-eyed peas
2, 15-ounce cans of diced tomato
1 diced onion
1 tablespoon minced garlic
1 tablespoon ginger paste
2 teaspoons garam masala
2 teaspoons cumin seeds
1 teaspoon sugar
1 teaspoon turmeric
1 teaspoon salt
½ teaspoon cayenne

<u>Directions:</u>

1. To quick-soak the beans, boil for 1 minute and then let them sit for at least 1 hour.
2. Preheat your Instant Pot and add a tiny bit of oil.
3. Add the onions and cook until they're soft.
4. Add cumin seeds and cook for 1 minute before adding ginger and garlic.

5. Drain the beans and add to the pot, along with the rest of the ingredients.
6. Close and seal the lid.
7. Select "manual," and cook for 7 minutes on high pressure.
8. When time is up, hit "cancel" and wait for the pressure to come down on its own.
9. Season.
10. Check the peas, and if they aren't tender enough, simmer for a little while.

Nutritional Info (⅛ recipe):

Total calories: 178
Protein: 11
Carbs: 32.8
Fiber: 5.8
Fat: 0

Italian Tofu Scramble

<u>Serves</u>: 4

<u>Time</u>: 12 minutes (5 minutes prep time, 7 minutes cook time)

This one-pot scramble is vegan Italy in a bowl. It's got garlic, tomatoes, Italian seasoning, and crumbled tofu, which takes on an egg-like texture. It only takes four minutes to cook, and then a quick-release.

<u>Ingredients:</u>

3 minced garlic cloves
1 sliced onion
1 cup diced carrots
1 block of extra firm tofu
1 can Italian-style diced tomatoes
¼ cup veggie broth
2 tablespoons jarred banana pepper rings
1 tablespoon Italian seasoning
1 teaspoon olive oil
1 teaspoon cumin
Ground black pepper

<u>Directions:</u>

1. Heat the olive oil in your Instant Pot on "sauté."
2. Add garlic, onion, and carrot for three minutes until the veggies are softened.
3. Crumble the tofu into the Pot.
4. Pour in veggie broth, peppers, tomatoes, and seasoning.
5. Mix before locking and sealing the lid.
6. Select "manual" and cook for 4 minutes on high pressure.
7. When time is up, hit "cancel" and quick-release.
8. Taste and season before serving.

Nutritional Info (¼ recipe):

Total calories: 135
Protein: 11
Carbs: 11
Fiber: 1
Fat: 7

Sweet Potato Spinach Curry w/ Chickpeas

Serves: 2
Time: 15 minutes (5 minutes prep time, 8-10 minutes cook time)

Chickpeas are a vegan superfood. They are packed with nutrition, including fiber and protein, and have a hearty texture. When paired with sweet potatoes, you get a very filling dinner bowl spiced with red onion, ginger, garam masala, and cinnamon.

Ingredients:

1 small can of drained chickpeas
1 ½ cups chopped sweet potatoes
3 chopped garlic cloves
2 cups chopped fresh spinach
1 ½ cups water
2 chopped tomatoes
½ chopped red onion
½-inch thumb of ginger, chopped
1 teaspoon olive oil
1 teaspoon coriander powder
½ teaspoon garam masala
¼ teaspoon cinnamon
Salt and pepper to taste
Squeeze of lemon

Directions:

1. Pour oil in your Instant Pot and heat on "sauté."
2. When the oil is hot, add the ginger, onion, and garlic.
3. When the onions are clear, add the spices and mix.
4. After 30 seconds, add tomatoes and mix to coat everything.
5. Add sweet potatoes, chickpeas, 1 ½ cups water, and a dash of salt.
6. Close and seal the lid.

7. Select "manual," and cook on high pressure for 8-10 minutes.
8. When time is up, hit "cancel" and do a natural pressure release.
9. Add the fresh spinach and stir so the heat wilts the leaves.
10. Taste and season more if necessary.
11. Serve with a squirt of fresh lemon.

Nutritional Info (½ recipe):

Total calories: 166.5
Protein: 6.8
Carbs: 32
Fiber: 7
Fat: 21

Easy Seitan Roast

<u>Serves</u>: 4

<u>Time</u>: 30 minutes (5 minutes prep time, 25 minutes cook time)

Seitan is a vegan meat substitute made from wheat gluten. It can be seasoned in a variety of ways, so you get rich flavors. This recipe uses plenty of herbs and salty ingredients. If you're gluten-intolerant or sensitive, stick to tofu, but if you aren't, try out this seitan roast in a flavorful simmering broth. You can pair seitan with any kind of vegan-friendly sauce or side.

Cooking Tip: When you slice seitan, it should have a meaty texture - not too soft, and not too chewy.

<u>Ingredients:</u>

1 ½ cups vital wheat gluten
1 cup veggie broth
⅓ cup tapioca flour
3 tablespoons nutritional yeast
2 tablespoons coconut aminos
1 tablespoon olive oil
1 tablespoon vegan Worcestershire sauce
1 teaspoon garlic powder
½ teaspoon dried thyme
½ teaspoon dried rosemary
¼ teaspoon black pepper
¼ teaspoon sea salt

3 cups veggie broth
2 cups water
¼ cup coconut aminos
2 tablespoons vegan Worcestershire
1 teaspoon onion powder

Directions:

1. Let's start with the first list of ingredients.
2. Whisk all the dry ingredients together.
3. In a separate bowl, mix the wet ones.
4. Pour the wet into the dry.
5. Fold first with a spoon, and then knead by hand for a few minutes.
6. Form into a round shape, pulling at the top, and then rolling under so it's smooth.
7. Shape into a more oblong loaf and roll tightly in cheesecloth, tying off the ends.
8. Put the roast in your Instant Pot.
9. Pour in all the ingredients in the second ingredient list.
10. Lock and seal the lid.
11. Select "manual," and cook on high pressure for 25 minutes.
12. When time is up, hit "cancel" and wait 10 minutes before quick-releasing the pressure.
13. Slice and serve!

Nutritional Info (¼ recipe):

Total calories: 451
Protein: 42
Carbs: 51
Fiber: 0
Fat: 4

Veggie Biryani

<u>Serves</u>: 8
<u>Time</u>: 30 minutes (15 minutes prep time, 15 minutes cook time)

Biryani is one of the most popular dishes in India. It's made from rice, and since so many people in India are vegetarian, many variations are vegetable-based. This particular biryani has cauliflower, potatoes, green beans, and carrots.

<u>Ingredients:</u>

2 cups rice
1 ½ cups water
1 ½ cups coconut milk
1 thinly-sliced onion
5 minced garlic cloves
1-inch thumb of ginger, grated
3 chopped small potatoes
1 small cauliflower's worth of florets
1 chopped carrot
1 cup green beans
¼ cup chopped mint leaves
¼ cup French's fried onions
1 tablespoon garam masala
1 tablespoon coconut oil
½ lemon, juiced

<u>Directions:</u>

1. Turn your Instant Pot to "sauté" and heat the oil.
2. When hot, add onion and mint leaves, and cook until the onions start to turn golden.
3. Add garlic and ginger.
4. After a minute, add the veggies and stir.

5. After 3 minutes, add fried onions.
6. Add the garam masala and coconut milk.
7. Pour in water and plenty of salt.
8. Lastly, add rice and lemon juice.
9. Mix everything before closing and sealing the lid.
10. Select "manual," and cook on high pressure for 3 minutes.
11. Hit "cancel" when time is up and wait for a natural release.
12. Stir with a fork before serving.

Nutritional Info (⅛ recipe):

Total calories: 215
Protein: 5
Carbs: 37
Fiber: 5.5
Fat: 6

Easy Ratatouille

<u>Serves</u>: 4
<u>Time</u>: 35 minutes (15 minutes prep time, 20 minutes cook time)

Ratatouille isn't just the name of a Pixar movie. It's a rustic eggplant dish originally from France; it's a vegan comfort food dream. There's also butternut squash, tomatoes, bell peppers, and plenty of garlic.

<u>Ingredients:</u>

3 cups diced butternut squash
2 cups chopped eggplant
4 chopped tomatoes
3 minced garlic cloves
2 chopped onions
1 chopped red bell pepper
1 chopped green bell pepper
1 tablespoon olive oil
2 teaspoons dried basil
1 teaspoon salt
½ teaspoon dried thyme
½ teaspoon black pepper

<u>Directions:</u>

1. Preheat your Instant Pot on the "sauté" setting and add oil.
2. When the oil is hot, cook the onion and garlic.
3. Add all your veggies, except tomatoes, and cook until they're soft.
4. Now you add the tomatoes.
5. Close and seal the pressure cooker lid.
6. Select "manual," and then five minutes on high pressure.
7. When time is up, hit "cancel" and let the pressure come down on its own.
8. Season and enjoy!

Nutritional Info (¼ recipe):

Total calories: 224
Protein: 9
Carbs: 38.2
Fiber: 8.6
Fat: 5.4

Jackfruit Sandwich "Meat"

<u>Serves</u>: 4
<u>Time</u>: 26 minutes (3 minutes prep time, 3 minutes cook time, 20 minutes release time)

You've heard of tempeh, tofu, and seitan as meat substitutes, but what about jackfruit? It has a very similar texture to meat, and when flavored with ingredients like cayenne, mustard seeds, garlic, and Worcestershire, it actually tastes a lot like the real thing! With this recipe, you can turn jackfruit into the perfect filling for BBQ sandwiches.

<u>Ingredients</u>:

17-ounces of rinsed and drained jackfruit (packed in water)
½-¾ cup water
¼ cup diced onion
3 tablespoons tomato paste
1 tablespoon minced garlic
1 tablespoon maple syrup
1 teaspoon olive oil
1 teaspoon apple cider vinegar
1 teaspoon vegan Worcestershire sauce
½ teaspoon cayenne pepper
½ teaspoon yellow mustard seeds
½ teaspoon salt
½ teaspoon black pepper

<u>Directions</u>:

1. Turn your Instant Pot to "sauté" and heat the oil.
2. When hot, add garlic and onion.
3. Cook for 3 minutes, or until the onion is soft.
4. Add the jackfruit, tomato paste, vinegar, Worcestershire, syrup, and seasonings.

5. Add just enough water to cover the jackfruit, and mix.
6. Close and seal the pressure cooker.
7. Select "manual," and cook on high pressure for 3 minutes.
8. Hit "cancel" when the timer goes off, and let the pressure come down naturally.
9. Open the lid and stir well.
10. With a fork, shred the fruit and serve on a toasted bun!

Nutritional Info (¼ recipe, jackfruit only):

Total calories: 79
Protein: 2
Carbs: 15
Fiber: 6
Fat: 1

Pressure-Cooker Penne Pasta

<u>Serves</u>: 2-4

<u>Time</u>: 25 minutes (5 minutes prep time, 20 minutes cook time)

Pressure cooking a pasta dinner is fast, but tastes like it's been simmering for hours. With a flavor base made from garlic, mushrooms, zucchini, onion, shallot, and herbs, the pasta cooks right in a homemade sauce.

<u>Ingredients</u>:

450 grams of penne pasta
3 minced garlic cloves
12 sliced white mushrooms
1 sliced zucchini
1 small sliced onion
1 small diced shallot
Pinch of dried oregano
Pinch of dried basil
Olive oil
Salt and pepper

2 cups water
1 cup veggie stock
Dash of sherry wine
½ cup tomato paste
2 tablespoons vegan-friendly light soy sauce

<u>Directions</u>:

1. Turn your Instant Pot to "sauté" to preheat the cooker.
2. Add oil and cook the shallot and onion.
3. Add salt and black pepper.
4. Stir until the veggies are browning.

5. Add the garlic and stir for half a minute.
6. Toss in the mushrooms, zucchini, and herbs.
7. Cook for a minute.
8. Time to make the sauce. Deglaze the pot with sherry.
9. Pour in veggie stock, 2 cups water, and soy sauce.
10. Put the pasta in the Pot and mix in tomato paste so it's totally covered.
11. Select "manual" and cook for 4 minutes on high pressure.
12. When time is up, hit "cancel" and wait 5 minutes before quick-releasing the pressure.
13. Mix and serve!

Tip: Deglazing is when you add a cooking liquid (like water, broth, or wine) to a pot and scrape off the bits of food that have stuck to the sides. These burned or browned bits add flavor.

Nutritional Info (¼ recipe):

Total calories: 235
Protein: 11
Carbs: 49
Fiber: 5
Fat: 1

Sun-Dried Tomato Pesto Pasta w/ Chard

<u>Serves</u>: 4
<u>Time</u>: 17 minutes (10 minutes prep time, 7 minutes cook time)

Sundried tomato pesto is bright and goes perfectly with chard, which is similar to spinach. Dill and red pepper flakes add complexity and heat. To make the dish healthier, go with whole-wheat pasta.

<u>Ingredients:</u>

1 pound whole-wheat elbow macaroni
4 sliced garlic cloves
3 minced garlic cloves
8 sun-dried tomatoes
6 thinly-sliced Swiss chard leaves
¼ cup walnuts
¼ cup + 1 teaspoon olive oil
¼ cup dill
1 teaspoon red pepper flakes
½ lemon, juiced
Salt to taste

<u>Directions:</u>

1. Put the tomatoes, dill, walnuts, minced garlic, ¼ cup olive oil, red pepper, lemon juice, and salt in a food processor.
2. Run until you get a rough paste.
3. Heat 1 teaspoon olive oil in your Instant Pot.
4. Add the sliced garlic and cook until they're golden.
5. Cook the chard until it wilts and the water is evaporated.
6. Add pasta and stir.
7. Pour in just enough water, so the pasta is covered.
8. Salt.
9. Close and seal the cooker. Select "manual," and cook on high

pressure for 3 minutes.
10. When time is up, hit "cancel," and let the pressure come down naturally.
11. When all the pressure is gone, add the pesto and stir well.
12. Season to taste.
13. Serve!

Nutritional Info (¼ recipe):

Total calories: 334
Protein: 9
Carbs: 37
Fiber: 6
Fat: 19

Black-Eyed Pea Cakes (Oil Free)

Serves: 4

Time: 1 hour, 40 minutes (1 hour soak time for peas, 10 minutes prep time, 30 minutes cook time)

These Nigerian savory cakes make an awesome light lunch and pack a whopping 29 grams of protein per 2-cake serving. These patties are made from black-eyed peas, onion, roasted red pepper, and spiced with Old Bay seasoning. These need to be steamed, so you'll be using the "Steam" program on your Instant Pot.

Ingredients:

1 cup dried black-eyed peas
1 chopped onion
1 roasted red pepper
¼ cup veggie broth
1 tablespoon tomato paste
1 ½ - 2 teaspoons Old Bay seasoning
1 teaspoon salt
¼ teaspoon white pepper

Directions:

1. Rinse and pick over the peas to take out any stones.
2. Soak in a large bowl of hot water, so there's two inches about the peas.
3. Soak for one hour and then drain.
4. Put the peas in a food processor and pulse until they're just broken.
5. Put the peas in the bowl and cover with more water.
6. Rub them, so their skins come off.
7. With the skins gone, the peas are white.
8. Put the peas back into the food processor with the onion, red pepper, tomato paste, and 2 tablespoons of broth.

9. Process until smooth.
10. Pour into bowl and add seasonings.
11. You want the mixture to be thick, but still pourable. Add more broth if necessary.
12. Pour 1 cup of water into your Instant Pot.
13. Grease 8 ramekins and pour ½ of the cake batter into each one.
14. Wrap in foil.
15. Lower the steamer basket (or trivet) into the cooker, and place the ramekins inside.
16. Close and seal lid.
17. Select the "steam" program and adjust time to 30 minutes.
18. When time is up, hit "cancel" and quick-release.
19. With a toothpick, check the cakes - a clean toothpick means they're ready.

Nutritional Info (2 cakes):

Total calories: 158
Protein: 29
Carbs: 9
Fiber: 5
Fat: 1

Vegan Mac + Cheese

<u>Serves:</u> 2
<u>Time:</u> 20 minutes (15 minutes prep time, 5 minutes cook time)

One of the foods vegans miss most is cheese. Luckily, vegan cheese is a thing, as is vegan butter. Chicken seasoning, a spice blend made with rosemary, thyme, paprika, and so on, adds a ton of flavor, so don't skip it!

<u>Ingredients:</u>

1 cup whole-wheat elbow pasta
1 cup diced onion
2 minced garlic cloves
2 tablespoons chicken seasoning
2 tablespoons vegan butter
2 tablespoons nutritional yeast
2-ounces shredded vegan cheese
Salt and ground pepper to taste

<u>Directions:</u>

1. Put the vegan butter in your pressure cooker and melt on "sautè."
2. Add the onion and garlic, and cook until the onion is clear.
3. Add the soy curls and chicken seasoning, and cook for 5 minutes.
4. Pour in the pasta, 2 cups of cool water, and nutritional yeast, and stir.
5. Select "manual," and cook on low pressure for 5 minutes, or high pressure for 3 minutes.
6. When time is up, hit "cancel" and quick-release the pressure.
7. Stir and stir in vegan cheese, salt, and pepper.
8. Before serving, let the mac 'n cheese sit for about 5 minutes.

Nutritional Info (½ recipe):

Total calories: 352
Protein: 10
Carbs: 42
Fiber: 4.5
Fat: 18

Chapter 8

Soups, Stews, and Chilis

Veggie-Quinoa Soup (Oil Free)

Serves: 6

Time: 20-40 minutes (2 minutes cook time, 20 minutes natural release)

This is the easiest soup you'll ever make. You literally just throw everything in the pressure cooker and step back. The quinoa adds a different flavor and consistency than the usual noodles

Cooking Tip: The reason the time range is so wide is because it can take between 15-20 minutes for the Instant Pot to reach pressure if you're using frozen veggies. Using boiling water helps with that, and if you use fresh veggies, it takes very little time to get to pressure)

Ingredients:

3 cups boiling water
2 bags of frozen mixed veggies (12-ounces each)
1 15-ounce can of white beans
1 15-ounce can of fire-roasted diced tomatoes
1 15-ounce can of pinto beans
¼ cup rinsed quinoa
1 tablespoon dried basil
1 tablespoon minced garlic
1 tablespoon hot sauce
½ tablespoon dried oregano
Dash of salt
Dash of black pepper

Directions:

1. Put everything in the Instant Pot and stir.
2. Close and seal the lid.
3. Select "manual," and set time to 2 minutes on high pressure.
4. When time is up, hit "cancel" and quick-release the pressure.

5. When all the pressure is gone, open the cooker and season to taste.
6. Serve!

Nutritional Info (1 ½ cups serving):

Total calories: 201
Protein: 11
Carbs: 37
Fiber: 11
Fat: 1.1

Turkish Soup

<u>Serves</u>: 1-2
<u>Time</u>: About 15 minutes (5 minutes prep time, 10 minutes cook time)

This simple soup has just the right amount of spices without being overwhelming for those with most delicate palates. It's thick and rich, but not too hearty. It would be a great option for lunch.

<u>Ingredients:</u>

1 cup red lentils
1 chopped carrot
1 chopped potato
1 chopped onion
½ cup celery
3 minced garlic cloves
½ tablespoon rice
3 teaspoons olive oil
½ teaspoon paprika
½ teaspoon coriander
Salt to taste

<u>Directions:</u>

1. Turn your Instant Pot to "sauté" and add oil.
2. While that heats up, prep your veggies.
3. When oil is hot, cook the garlic for a few minutes until fragrant.
4. Rinse off the rice and lentils, and put them in the pressure cooker.
5. Add 2 ½ cups of water, paprika, salt, and veggies.
6. Close and seal the lid.
7. Select "manual" and cook on high pressure for 10 minutes.
8. When time is up, hit "cancel," and quick-release.
9. Let the mixture cool for a little while before pureeing in a blender.
10. Serve!

Nutritional Info (½ recipe):

Total calories: 531
Protein: 29
Carbs: 73
Fiber: 10
Fat: 9

Lentil Soup with Cumin and Coriander

<u>Serves</u>: 8

<u>Time</u>: 30 minutes (10 minutes prep time, 20 minutes cook time)

If you need a hot meal for a crowd, try out this lentil soup spiced with cumin and coriander. You can use brown or green lentils (I use brown), and you only need a few good veggies (potatoes, carrots, onion, and celery) to add tons of depth and flavor.

<u>Ingredients:</u>

8 cups of veggie broth
2 cups uncooked brown lentils
2 sliced carrots
2 cubed big Yukon gold potatoes
2 bay leaves
2 minced garlic cloves
1 chopped onion
1 chopped celery rib
1 teaspoon ground coriander
½ teaspoon ground cumin
Black pepper to taste

<u>Directions:</u>

1. First, pick through the lentils and throw out any stones, and then rinse.
2. Pour the broth in your Instant Pot and turn to "sauté" so it heats up.
3. Prep the veggies.
4. Add to the pressure cooker, along with everything else.
5. Close and seal the pressure cooker.
6. Select "manual," and cook on high pressure for 10 minutes.
7. After hitting "cancel," wait for 5 minutes before quick-releasing.

8. Check the tenderness of the lentils and potatoes.
9. If not done, turn the pot back on "sauté" and finish cooking with the lid on, but not sealed or at pressure.
10. Pick out the bay leaves, and salt to taste.
11. Serve with a squirt of lemon juice.

<u>Nutritional Info (⅛ recipe):</u>

Total calories: 228
Protein: 14.4
Carbs: 41
Fiber: 17
Fat: 0

Miso Soup

<u>Serves</u>: 4
<u>Time</u>: About 6 minutes

A lot of these recipes are Indian, because of the pressure cooker's popularity, so if you want to shake things up a bit, let's travel over to Japan. Miso soup is awesome for when you're feeling blue in the dead of winter. It's like a vegan's chicken noodle soup for the soul.

Cooking Tip: Wakame flakes are dehydrated type of seaweed, and can be found on Amazon or your local Asian market.

<u>Ingredients:</u>

4 cups water
1 cup cubed silken tofu
2 chopped carrots
2 chopped celery stalks
1 sliced onion
2 tablespoons miso paste
Dash of vegan-friendly soy sauce

<u>Directions:</u>

1. Put the carrots, onion, celery, tofu, wakame, and water in your Instant Pot.
2. Close and seal.
3. Select "manual," and cook on high pressure for 6 minutes.
4. When time is up, hit "cancel" and quick-release.
5. Open the lid and ladle out one cup of broth.
6. Add the miso paste to this broth and whisk until completely dissolved.
7. Pour back into pot and stir.
8. Season with soy sauce and serve!

Nutritional Info (¼ recipe):

Total calories: 74
Protein: 4
Carbs: 9
Fiber: 1
Fat: 2

Barley + Winter Vegetable Soup

<u>Serves</u>: 6-8
<u>Time</u>: About 25 minutes (5 minutes prep time, 8 minutes cook time, 10 minutes natural release)

For a hearty soup using in-season ingredients, you can't beat barley and winter veggies. Winter veggie options include turnips, sweet potato, rutabaga, or celery root. This recipe makes up to 8 servings, so you can eat it all week.

<u>Ingredients:</u>

6 cups veggie broth
1-3 cups water
2 cups chopped winter veggie
1 ½ cups chopped carrots
1 cup sliced onions
1 cup peeled, chopped parsnip
1 cup pearled barley
1 chopped potato
½ cup chopped celery
1-2 tablespoons tamari
1 tablespoon olive oil
1 tablespoon miso (dissolved in 3 tablespoons water)
Salt and pepper to taste

<u>Directions:</u>

1. Pour oil into your Instant Pot and heat on the "sauté" setting.
2. When hot, cook celery, carrots, and onions until the onions are browning.
3. Pour in the broth, and add potato, tamari, parsnip, and barley.
4. Close and seal the lid.
5. Select "manual" and cook on high pressure for 8 minutes.

6. When time is up, hit "cancel" and let the pressure come down naturally.
7. Check the barley, and if it isn't cooked through, bring the pot back to pressure for 3-5 minutes.
8. When ready, add the miso (dissolved in water).
9. Season and serve!

Nutritional Info (⅛ recipe):

Total calories: 233
Protein: 4
Carbs: 29
Fiber: 7
Fat: 2

Split-Pea Soup

<u>Serves</u>: 6

<u>Time</u>: 55 minutes (10 minutes prep time, 45 minutes cook time)

Split peas are commonly-paired with ham, but to veganize the classic soup, you use spices like smoked paprika, thyme, black pepper, and a bay leaf. Other aromatics like celery, carrots, and onion add even more flavor.

<u>Ingredients:</u>

6 cups veggie broth
1 pound of split peas
3 diced carrots
3 diced celery ribs
1 diced yellow onion
2 minced garlic cloves
2 tablespoons coconut oil
1 bay leaf
½ tablespoon smoked paprika
¼ teaspoon dried thyme
Black pepper

<u>Directions:</u>

1. Prep your veggies.
2. Put everything in your Instant Pot and seal the lid.
3. Select "manual," then cook on high pressure for 15 minutes.
4. Hit "cancel" when time is up, and wait for the pressure to come down on its own.
5. When the pressure is gone, open and stir the soup.
6. Season to taste.

Nutritional Info (⅙ recipe):

Total calories: 180
Protein: 12
Carbs: 32
Fiber: 13
Fat: 1

Mexican Baked Potato Soup (Oil Free)

<u>Serves</u>: 4

<u>Time</u>: 35 minutes (5 minutes prep time, 10 minutes cook time, 20 minutes natural release)

Baked potatoes are great, but they can get a bit boring after a while. How about you turn them into a creamy soup? Just add veggie broth, a few extra ingredients like salsa and jalapenos, and season it all with garlic, cumin, and oregano, and you've got a delicious hot meal that's vegan and oil-free!

<u>Ingredients:</u>

4 cups veggie broth
4 cups diced potatoes
4 diced garlic cloves
1 diced onion
½ cup salsa
½ cup nutritional yeast
⅛ cup seeded jalapeno peppers
1 teaspoon cumin
¼ teaspoon oregano
Black pepper to taste

<u>Directions:</u>

1. Turn your Instant Pot to "sauté."
2. When hot, add the onion, jalapeno, and garlic.
3. Stir until browning.
4. Hit "cancel" before adding potatoes, salsa, cumin, and oregano, and pouring the broth over everything.
5. Stir.
6. Close and seal the lid.
7. Select "manual," and cook for 10 minutes on high pressure.

8. When time is up, hit "cancel" and wait for the pressure to come down on its own.
9. After 20 minutes, release any leftover pressure.
10. To make the soup creamy, run through a blender.
11. Add nutritional yeast and pepper.
12. Serve!

Nutritional Info (¼ recipe):

Total calories: 196
Protein: 10
Carbs: 30
Fiber: 4
Fat: 0

Red Curry-Coconut Milk Soup (Oil Free)

<u>Serves</u>: 4

<u>Time</u>: 21 minutes (5 minutes prep time, 6 minutes cook time, 10 minutes natural release)

The heat from this recipe's red curry paste and red pepper is smoothed out with coconut milk, which also makes this soup creamy and lovely. Red lentils and spinach add a ton of nutritional value, and if there are leftovers, the soup freezes well for future meals to come.

<u>Ingredients:</u>

2 cups veggie broth
1 ½ cups red lentils
1, 15-ounce can of coconut milk
1, 14-ounce can of diced tomatoes (with liquid)
1 diced onion
3 minced garlic cloves
2 tablespoons red curry paste
⅛ teaspoon ground ginger
Dash of red pepper
Handful of spinach

<u>Directions:</u>

1. Preheat your Instant Pot on the "sauté" setting.
2. When hot, cook onion and garlic until they're beginning to brown.
3. Hit "cancel."
4. Add the curry paste, ground ginger, and red pepper.
5. Stir to coat the onion and garlic in spices.
6. Pour in the diced tomatoes with their liquid, coconut milk, veggie broth, and lentils.
7. Stir before closing and sealing the lid.
8. Hit "manual" and cook for 6 minutes on high pressure.

9. When time is up, hit "cancel" and wait for the pressure to come down on its own.
10. When the pressure it all gone, throw in the spinach and serve when the leaves have wilted.

Nutritional Info (¼ recipe):

Total calories: 553
Protein: 22
Carbs: 60
Fiber: 7
Fat: 24

Weeknight Three-Bean Chili (Oil Free)

Serves: 6-8
Time: 26 minutes (10 minutes prep time, 6 minutes cook time, 10 minutes natural release)

This is probably one of the easiest and fastest chili recipes you could make. By using canned beans, you negate the need for soak time, and cut the cooking time in half. The result is a protein and fiber-hearty meal with lot of aromatics and spice.

Ingredients:

3 ½ cups veggie broth
1 can black beans
1 can red beans
1 can pinto beans
1, 14.5-ounce can diced tomatoes
1, 14.5-ounce can tomato sauce
2 cups chopped onion
¾ cup chopped carrots
¼ cup chopped celery
1 chopped red bell pepper
2 tablespoons mild chili powder
1 tablespoon minced garlic
1 ½ teaspoons ground cumin
1 ½ teaspoons dried oregano
1 teaspoon smoked paprika

Directions:

1. Rinse and drain the canned beans.
2. Heat your Instant Pot before throwing in the onion and garlic to sauté for 5 minutes or so.
3. Add the rest of the ingredients, except the tomatoes and tomato

sauce.
4. Stir.
5. Close and seal the lid.
6. Select "manual" and cook on high pressure for 6 minutes.
7. When time is up, hit "cancel" and let the pressure come down naturally.
8. When the pressure is gone, stir in the tomato sauce and diced tomatoes.
9. If you want a thicker chili, spoon out 1-2 cups of the chili and blend before returning to the pot.
10. Serve with fresh parsley if desired.

Nutritional Info (⅛ recipe):

Total calories: 167
Protein: 10
Carbs: 32
Fiber: 11.5
Fat: 1

Root Veggie Soup

<u>Serves</u>: 8
<u>Time</u>: 1 hour, 30 minutes (10 minutes prep time, 30 minutes cook time, 50 minutes natural release)

Veggies from beneath the ground are very healthy. The vegetables of choice in this soup are potatoes, carrots, and onions. There's also some canned tomatoes and seasonings, of course, but the true stars are those nutrition-packed root vegetables.

<u>Ingredients:</u>

7 cups veggie broth
6 cups peeled and chopped russet potatoes
3 cups peeled and chopped carrots
1 cup Italian-style tomatoes (canned)
1 cup chopped yellow onion
½ cup coconut oil
2 tablespoons garlic powder
1 tablespoon mild chili powder
1 tablespoon salt

<u>Directions:</u>

1. Pour everything in your Instant Pot.
2. Stir before closing and sealing the lid.
3. Select "Soup" and adjust time to 30 minutes.
4. When time is up, hit "cancel" and wait for a natural pressure release.
5. To make the soup creamy, blend until smooth.
6. Taste and season more if necessary.

Nutritional Info (⅛ recipe):

Total calories: 256
Protein: 4
Carbs: 31
Fiber: 4
Fat: 14

Spicy Chili w/ Red Lentils (Oil Free)

Serves: 5
Time: 47 minutes (15 minutes prep time, 17 minutes cook time, 15 minutes natural release)

We can't get enough of red lentils! In this recipe, they're part of a spicy chili with just a hint of sweetness from some brown sugar and apple cider vinegar. The heat comes from a combination of cayenne, paprika, and chili powder. To make this a full meal that can serve 4-5, serve over rice.

Ingredients:

7 cups water
2 cups red lentils
2 diced red peppers
1 diced onion
14-ounce can of diced tomatoes
5 minced garlic cloves
¼ cup brown sugar
6-ounce can of tomato paste
2 tablespoons apple cider vinegar
1 tablespoon paprika
1 tablespoon chili powder
1 teaspoon cayenne

Directions:

1. Prep your ingredients.
2. Throw everything in the Instant Pot and seal the lid.
3. Select "manual" and cook for 17 minutes on high pressure.
4. When the timer beeps, hit "cancel" and wait 15 minutes before quick-releasing.
5. Stir and serve over rice!

Nutritional Info (⅕ recipe, just chili):

Total calories: 420
Protein: 24
Carbs: 76
Fiber: 6
Fat: 2

Guacamole Soup (Oil Free)

<u>Serves</u>: 4

<u>Time</u>: 35 minutes (10 minutes prep time, 10 minutes cook time, 15 minutes natural release)

Creamy and warm, this avocado-based soup is the perfect accompaniment to some high-quality, crusty bread. Since avocados are relatively bland, the sweetness from the agave syrup, spiciness of the habanero, and earthiness of the cumin add layer upon layer of flavor.

<u>Ingredients:</u>

4 cups veggie stock
3 smashed, ripe avocados
1 chopped onion
3 minced garlic cloves
1 tablespoon ground cumin
1 bay leaf
1 teaspoon oregano
⅛ seeded and chopped small habanero
1-2 teaspoons agave syrup
Salt and pepper to taste

<u>Directions:</u>

1. Turn your Instant Pot to "sauté."
2. When hot, cook the onions and garlic for about 5 minutes, or until fragrant, and the onions are clear.
3. Add the rest of the ingredients (minus the agave) to the pot.
4. Select "manual," and cook on high pressure for 10 minutes.
5. When done, hit "cancel" and wait for the pressure to come down by itself.
6. When all the pressure is gone, open the lid and pick out the bay leaf.
7. Blend the soup till smooth before adding the agave syrup and a

squirt of lime juice.

8. Season more to taste if necessary before serving.

Nutritional Info (¼ recipe):

Total calories: 239
Protein: 3
Carbs: 18
Fiber: 10
Fat: 17

"Meaty" Seitan Stew

<u>Serves</u>: 6-8

<u>Time</u>: 10 minutes

You learned how to make seitan back in the "One-Pot" chapter, and this recipe teaches you how to whip up a hearty stew with a seitan roast. With potatoes, carrots, corn, and green beans, it's a vegan version of a meaty classic.

<u>Ingredients:</u>

4 cups veggie broth
2 cups cubed seitan
6 quartered baby potatoes
3 chopped carrots
1, 15-ounce can of corn
1, 15-ounce can of green beans
1 chopped sweet onion
2 bay leaves
2 tablespoons vegan-friendly Worcestershire sauce
2 tablespoons arrowroot powder
1 tablespoon tomato paste
1 tablespoon cumin
1 teaspoon garlic powder
1 teaspoon onion powder
1 teaspoon paprika

<u>Directions:</u>

1. Dissolve the arrowroot powder in a little bit of water.
2. Pour (along with everything else) in the Instant Pot and stir.
3. Close and seal the lid.
4. Select "manual," and cook on high pressure for 10 minutes.
5. When the timer beeps, press "cancel" and then quick-release.

6. Pick out the bay leaves before serving.
7. Add some black pepper if desired.

Nutritional Info (⅛ recipe):

Total calories: 213
Protein: 19
Carbs: 29
Fiber: 3
Fat: 2

Classic (Vegan) Chili

Serves: 8

Time: 37 minutes (30 minutes prep time, 7 minutes cook time)

If you need a big hearty meal for a lot of people, this vegan chili is the perfect recipe. It's vegan-friendly while still being accessible to non-vegans, and if there are leftovers, it freezes really well. It's also incredibly quick at just under 40 minutes, so you don't need to spend all day cooking.

Ingredients:

6 cups tomato juice
7 cups canned kidney beans
2 cups textured soy protein (Bob's Red Mill)
2 cans diced tomatoes
1 cup water
5 minced garlic cloves
1 diced onion
2 tablespoons veggie oil
1 tablespoon + 1 teaspoon chili powder
1 teaspoon garlic powder
1 teaspoon sea salt
½ teaspoon cumin
Salt to taste

Directions:

1. Turn your Instant Pot to "sauté" and heat the veggie oil.
2. When hot, cook onions until they're soft and about to become clear.
3. Add the garlic and cook for a minute or so.
4. Scoop out the onions and garlic.
5. Add the tomato juice and seasonings.
6. Puree the onion/garlic mixture before returning to the pot.
7. Add the rest of the ingredients.

8. Close and seal the lid.
9. Hit "soup" and adjust time to 7 minutes.
10. When time is up, hit "cancel" and quick-release.
11. Taste and season before serving!

Nutritional Info (⅛ recipe):

Total calories: 331
Protein: 25
Carbs: 51
Fiber: 12
Fat: 5

Creamy Broccoli Soup with "Chicken" and Rice

<u>Serves</u>: 8-10

<u>Time</u>: 36 minutes (30 minutes prep time, 6 minutes cook time)

This soup uses a lot of vegan versions of ingredients, like vegan chicken and a bouillon cube. Some good brands include Beyond Meat, Better Than Bouillon, Edward & Sons, and Orrington Farms. You add the chicken and rice after pureeing the broccoli-and-cauliflower soup, so there's some texture.

<u>Ingredients:</u>

2 boxes of mushroom broth
2 bunches' worth of broccoli florets
1 head's worth of cauliflower florets
1 medium-sized, diced Yukon Gold potato
2 cups cooked brown rice
1 package of vegan chicken strips
1 vegan, chicken-flavored bouillon cube
1 cup water
1 cup unsweetened almond milk
3 minced garlic cloves
1 diced white onion
2 tablespoons tamari
1 tablespoon veggie oil
Dash of salt
Dash of black pepper

<u>Directions:</u>

1. Heat the oil in your Instant Pot on the "sauté" setting.
2. Toss in the onion and cook until soft.
3. Add garlic and cook for another minute or so.

4. Hit "cancel" and add the broccoli, cauliflower, and potato.
5. Season with the tamari, salt, pepper, and bouillon cube.
6. Pour in the liquids (water, milk, and broth) and stir.
7. Close and seal the lid.
8. Select "manual," and adjust time to 6 minutes on high pressure.
9. After hitting "cancel" when time is up, quick-release the pressure.
10. Puree when the soup has cooled a little.
11. Before serving, add the vegan chicken strips and cooked rice.

Nutritional Info (1/10 recipe):

Total calories: 193
Protein: 8
Carbs: 28
Fiber: 5
Fat: 5

Chicken(less) Soup (Oil Free)

<u>Serves</u>: 4
<u>Time</u>: 20 minutes (10 minutes prep time, 10 minutes cook time)

Craving chicken soup? You can get the flavor of chicken using tofu and a seasoning blend full of spices usually paired with poultry. The hot and comforting dish only takes 10 minutes under pressure followed by a quick-release, so you can get your fix in a flash.

<u>Ingredients:</u>

6 cups hot water
1 cup diced potatoes
2 diced carrots
1 minced onion
1 diced celery rib
¾ cup cubed, extra-firm tofu
2 bay leaves
2 tablespoons seasoning blend*
2 teaspoons minced garlic
1 teaspoon salt
⅛ teaspoon dried thyme

*¾ cup nutritional yeast flakes
1 ½ tablespoons onion powder
1 tablespoon dried basil
1 tablespoon dried oregano
1 tablespoon dried parsley
1 teaspoon salt
½ teaspoon celery seed
¼ teaspoon white pepper

Cooking Tip: You can use your seasoning blend for any dish that requires a chicken-like flavor! About ½ tablespoon per 1 cup of hot

water will produce a good flavor.

Directions:

1. To make your seasoning blend, put everything in a blender and process until it has become a fine powder. Don't breathe it in.
2. Mix 2 tablespoons into your water and set aside.
3. Turn your Instant Pot to "sauté" and cook the onion until brown.
4. Add garlic and cook for another minute.
5. Add the rest of the ingredients, including the seasoned water.
6. Close and seal the lid.
7. Select "soup" and adjust time to 10 minutes.
8. When time is up, hit "cancel" to turn off the cooker, and then quick-release.
9. Serve!

Nutritional Info (¼ recipe):

Total calories: 90
Protein: 6
Carbs: 15
Fiber: 3
Fat: 2

Chapter 9

Sides + Snacks

Fava Bean Dip

Makes: 1 ½ cups
Time: 27 minutes (5 minutes prep time, 12 minutes cook time, 10 minutes natural release) + overnight bean soak

Homemade bean dip is very easy and delicious with fresh-cut veggies, pita, or pita chips. This recipe produces 1 ½ cups, so make this for you and a movie-night buddy to share. Keep in mind that you'll need to soak the beans overnight before using the Instant Pot.

Ingredients:

3 cups water
2 cups soaked split fava beans
2 crushed garlic cloves
2 tablespoons veggie oil
1 tablespoon olive oil
1 zested and juiced lemon
2 teaspoons tahini
2 teaspoons cumin
1 teaspoon harissa
1 teaspoon paprika
Salt to taste

Directions:

1. The night before, soak the fava beans and drain the fava beans before beginning the recipe.
2. Preheat your Instant Pot.
3. Add garlic when hot and cook until they become golden.
4. Add beans, veggie oil, and 3 cups of water.
5. Close and seal the lid.
6. Select "manual" and cook on high pressure for 12 minutes.
7. When time is up, hit "cancel" and wait 10 minutes before quick-

releasing any remaining pressure.
8. Drain the cooking liquid from the pressure cooker, leaving about 1 cup.
9. Toss in the tahini, cumin, harissa, and lemon zest.
10. Puree until smooth.
11. Salt and blend again.
12. Serve with a drizzle of olive oil and dash of paprika.

Nutritional Info (½ recipe):

Total calories: 415
Protein: 15
Carbs: 31
Fiber: 7
Fat: 26

Mango Chutney

<u>Makes</u>: 2 cups
<u>Time</u>: 25 minutes (5 minutes prep time, 20 minutes cook time)

Mango chutney is a spicy-sweet condiment that can be used in everything from curries to sandwiches with avocado and alfalfa sprouts. It would also be awesome on a veggie burger!

Cooking Tip: Refrigerated chutney will last up to a month, while in the freezer, it can last up to a year.

<u>Ingredients:</u>

2 big, diced mangos
1 cored and diced apple
1 ¼ cups apple cider vinegar
1 ¼ cups raw sugar
¼ cup raisins
1 chopped shallot
2 tablespoons finely-diced ginger
1 tablespoon veggie oil
2 teaspoons salt
½ teaspoon red pepper flakes
¼ teaspoon cardamom powder
⅛ teaspoons cinnamon

<u>Directions:</u>

1. Preheat your Instant Pot.
2. When hot, add the oil and cook shallots and ginger until the shallot is soft.
3. Add cinnamon, chili powder, and cardamom and cook for 1 minute.
4. Add the rest of the ingredients and mix.
5. When the sugar has melted, close and seal the lid.

6. Select "manual" and cook for 7 minutes on high pressure.
7. When the beeper sounds, hit "cancel" and wait for the pressure to come down on its own.
8. Turn the pot back to "sauté" with the lid off until the chutney has a jam-like texture.
9. When it starts to thicken, turn the cooker to the "keep warm" setting.
10. When you get the texture you want, move the chutney to glass jars and close.
11. When the contents are cool, move to the fridge.

Nutritional Info (1 tablespoon):

Total calories: 78.2
Protein: .9
Carbs: 18.3
Fiber: 1
Fat: .3

Mushroom Risotto

<u>Serves</u>: 4-6

<u>Time</u>: 30 minutes (10 minutes prep time, 20 minutes cook time)

Rich roasted mushrooms, vegan butter, and umami miso paste make for one delicious risotto. It's so good and satisfying you could eat this as a main course if you wanted, though a small amount as a side dish with stuffed eggplant would also be good.

<u>Ingredients:</u>

4 cups veggie stock
1 ½ pounds mixed, chopped mushrooms
1 ounce dried porcini mushrooms
2 cups Arborio rice
1 cup chopped yellow onion
¾ cups dry white wine
4 tablespoons olive oil
4 tablespoons vegan butter
1 tablespoon miso paste
2 teaspoons soy sauce
2 teaspoons minced garlic
½ cup chopped herbs

<u>Directions:</u>

1. Microwave the dried mushrooms in broth for 5 minutes.
2. Chop the porcini and set aside for now. Keep the broth separate.
3. Heat olive oil in your Instant Pot.
4. Add the fresh mixed mushrooms and cook for about 8 minutes until brown.
5. Season with salt and pepper.
6. Add the onion, garlic, porcini, and butter.
7. Stir until the onions are soft.

8. Add the rice and stir to coat in oil.
9. When toasty after 3-4 minutes, add the soy sauce and miso paste.
10. Pour in the wine and cook for 2 minutes.
11. Pour the broth through a strainer into the pot and deglaze.
12. Close and seal the pressure cooker.
13. Select "manual" and cook on high pressure for 5 minutes.
14. When the beeper goes off, hit "cancel" and quick-release.
15. Open the lid and stir. If it's not thick enough, turn on the "sauté" program and stir.
16. Add herbs and season with salt and pepper before serving.

Nutritional Info (⅙ recipe):

Total calories: 431
Protein: 10
Carbs: 58
Fiber: 8
Fat: 17

Smoky Lima Beans

<u>Serves</u>: 12
<u>Time</u>: 1 hour, 10 minutes (25 minutes cook time, 5 minutes natural pressure release, 10 minutes boil time, 20-30 minutes simmer time)

For smoky, campfire-ready lima beans, all you need is the right seasonings. No meat at all. For the liquid smoke, Colgin is a good vegan brand, but most brands should be vegan. Just take a look at the ingredient list to be sure. To make enough beans for 12 people, you'll need an 8-quart cooker.

<u>Ingredients</u>:

12 cups water
2 pounds dry large lima beans
⅛ cup Colgin liquid smoke
1 teaspoon onion powder
1 teaspoon garlic powder
Salt and pepper to taste

<u>Directions</u>:

1. Rinse beans before putting into the IP with your water.
2. Add onion and garlic powder, and seal the lid.
3. Hit "Bean" and adjust to 25 minutes.
4. When time is up, wait 5 minutes and then quick-release the pressure.
5. Add salt and liquid smoke.
6. Taste and add more seasonings if necessary.
7. Hit "sauté" and bring to a boil for 10 minutes.
8. Then, hit "cancel."
9. Turn back to "sauté" and simmer for 20-30 minutes, until thickened.

Nutritional Info (½ cup per serving):
Total calories: 213
Protein: 16
Carbs: 40
Fat: 0
Fiber: 7

Polenta with Herbs (Oil Free)

Serves: 4-6
Time: 20 minutes (5 minutes prep time, 5 minutes cook time, 10 minutes natural release)

Polenta can be tricky to get just right, but it's easy when you use the Instant Pot. This is a simple recipe with simple, rustic flavors coming from lots of fresh herbs, onion, and garlic. You can use dried; just remember to reduce the amount by about half, since dried herbs have more concentrated flavor.

Ingredients:

3 cups veggie broth
1 cup water
1 cup coarse-ground polenta
1 large minced onion
3 tablespoons fresh, chopped thyme
2 tablespoons fresh, chopped Italian parsley
1 tablespoon minced garlic
1 teaspoon fresh, chopped sage
Salt and pepper to taste

Directions:

1. Preheat your cooker and dry-sautè the onion for about a minute.
2. Add the minced garlic and cook for one more minute.
3. Pour in the broth, along with the thyme, parsley, and sage.
4. Stir.
5. Sprinkle the polenta in the pot, but don't stir it in.
6. Close and seal the lid.
7. Select "manual" and cook on high pressure for 5 minutes.
8. When the timer beeps, hit "cancel" and wait 10 minutes.
9. Pick out the bay leaf.

10. Using a whisk, stir the polenta to smooth it. If it's thin, simmer on the "sauté" setting until it reaches the consistency you like.
11. Season to taste with salt and pepper before serving.

Nutritional Info (⅙ recipe):

Total calories: 103
Protein: 0
Carbs: 3
Fat: 0
Fiber: 2

Sweet Thai Coconut Rice (Oil Free)

<u>Serves:</u> 4

<u>Time:</u> About 23 minutes (3 minutes cook time, 10 minutes natural release, 5-10 minutes rest time)

This 5-ingredient side dish can be easily adapted into a dessert by adding more sugar, but it also makes a tasty afternoon snack when you're craving something a little sweet.

<u>Ingredients:</u>

1 ½ cups water
1 cup Thai sweet rice
½ can full-fat coconut milk
2 tablespoons sugar
Dash of salt

<u>Directions:</u>

1. Mix rice and water in your Instant Pot.
2. Select "manual" and cook for just 3 minutes on high pressure.
3. When time is up, hit "cancel" and wait 10 minutes for a natural release.
4. In the meanwhile, heat coconut milk, sugar, and salt in a saucepan.
5. When the sugar has melted, remove from the heat.
6. When the cooker has released its pressure, mix the coconut milk mixture into your rice and stir.
7. Put the lid back on and let it rest 5-10 minutes, without returning it to pressure.
8. Serve and enjoy!

Nutritional Info (¼ recipe):
Total calories: 269
Protein: 4
Carbs: 47
Fiber: 0
Fat: 8

Porcini Mushroom Pate

<u>Serves</u>: 6-8

<u>Time</u>: 2 hours, 21 minutes (1o minutes prep time, 11 minutes cook time, 2 hours chill time)

Pate is traditionally made with very fatty meat, which is a big no-no for vegans for a variety of reasons. "True" pate is even illegal in many countries because of animal cruelty laws. Luckily, there's none of that going on in this recipe. You use both fresh and dried mushrooms for a rich, earthy spread seasoned simply with shallot, salt, pepper, and a bay leaf.

<u>Ingredients:</u>

1 pound sliced fresh cremini mushrooms
30 grams rinsed dry porcini mushrooms
1 cup boiling water
¼ cup dry white wine
1 bay leaf
1 sliced shallot
2 tablespoons olive oil
1 ½ teaspoons salt
½ teaspoon white pepper

<u>Directions:</u>

1. Place dry porcini mushrooms in a bowl and pour over boiling water.
2. Cover and set aside for now.
3. Heat 1 tablespoon of oil in your Instant Pot.
4. When hot, cook the shallot until soft.
5. Add cremini mushrooms and cook until they've turned golden.
6. Deglaze with the wine, and let it evaporate.
7. Pour in the porcini mushrooms along with their water.
8. Toss in salt, pepper, and the bay leaf.
9. Close and seal the lid.

10. Select "manual" and cook on high pressure for 10 minutes.
11. When the timer beeps, hit "cancel" and quick-release.
12. Pick out the bay leaf before adding the last tablespoon of oil.
13. Puree mixture until smooth.
14. Refrigerate in a closed container for at least 2 hours before eating.

Nutritional Info (⅛ recipe):

Total calories: 70
Protein: 4
Carbs: 6
Fiber: 2.6
Fat: 4

Japanese-Pumpkin Rice

Serves: 2-4

Time: 22 minutes (5 minutes prep time, 7 minutes cook time, 10 minutes natural release)

This unique rice dish is *so* easy to make. There's no sautéing or multiple cooking steps, you literally just put everything in your Instant Pot, cook, and eat! Japanese pumpkin is known in America as Kabocha squash. It's basically a cross between the sweetness of a pumpkin and a sweet potato.

Ingredients:

2 cups cubed Kabocha squash
2 cups (360 ml) rice
1 ½ cups water
4 drops sesame oil
1 tablespoon cooking sake
1 teaspoon salt

Directions:

1. Mix rice, water, sake, sesame oil, and salt in your Instant Pot.
2. Add the squash.
3. Close and seal the lid.
4. Select "manual," and cook on high pressure for 7 minutes.
5. When time is up, hit "cancel" and wait 10 minutes.
6. Quick-release any remaining pressure.
7. Stir and serve!

Nutritional Info (¼ recipe):

Total calories: 355
Protein: 9
Carbs: 82
Fiber: 6
Fat: 4

Thai Chickpeas (Oil Free)

Serves: 6-8
Time: 18 minutes + overnight chickpea soak

This chickpea side dish has all the flavors - sweet, salty, spicy, savory. The coconut milk creates a gorgeous, creamy sauce that's sweetened with the potatoes, salted with the tamari, spiced with curry powder, and freshened up with herbs. It's perfect for cooked chickpeas.

Ingredients:

1 ½ cups soaked chickpeas
3 cups coconut milk
¾ pound peeled and chopped sweet potatoes
1 cup chopped canned plum tomatoes
1 tablespoon mild curry powder
¼ cup fresh, minced coriander
½ cup fresh, minced basil
1 tablespoon tamari
1 teaspoon minced garlic

Directions:

1. The night before, soak the chickpeas in water on the counter.
2. When ready, drain and rinse.
3. Add chickpeas to your Instant Pot, along with garlic, potatoes, tomatoes, curry powder, coriander, and coconut milk.
4. Close and seal the lid.
5. Select "manual" and cook on high pressure for 18 minutes.
6. When time is up, hit "cancel" and carefully quick-release.
7. If the chickpeas are not done, put the lid back on and simmer.
8. Add basil and tamari.
9. With a wooden spoon, break up the sweet potatoes and stir, so you get a sauce.

10. Serve as is or with rice.

Nutritional Info (⅛ recipe):

Total calories: 104
Protein: 2
Carbs: 15
Fiber: 6.5
Fat: 4

Easy Garlic-Roasted Potatoes

Serves: 4

Time: 27 minutes (10 minutes prep time, 7 minutes cook time, 10 minutes natural release)

I have not met a person who doesn't like a good potato side dish. This recipe is for baby potatoes roasted in your pressure cooker. The roasting effect is created by browning the outside of the raw potatoes in oil before cooking under pressure. This keeps the skin crisp.

Ingredients:

2 pounds baby potatoes
4 tablespoons veggie oil
3 garlic cloves
½ cup veggie stock
1 rosemary sprig
Salt and pepper to taste

Directions:

1. Preheat your Instant Pot.
2. When hot, add oil.
3. When the oil is hot, put in your potatoes, garlic, and rosemary.
4. Stir to coat the potatoes in oil, and brown on all sides.
5. After 8-10 minutes of browning, stop stirring, and pierce the middle of each potato with a knife.
6. Pour in the stock.
7. Close and seal the lid.
8. Select "manual" and cook on high pressure for 7 minutes.
9. When time is up, hit "cancel" and wait 10 minutes before quick-releasing any leftover pressure.
10. Season before serving!

Nutritional Info (¼ recipe):

Total calories: 336
Protein: 5
Carbs: 49
Fiber: 7
Fat: 14

2-Minute Steamed Asparagus

<u>Serves</u>: 3-4
<u>Time</u>: 2 minutes

Get fresh asparagus when it's in season from February through June, and steam up a batch in your pressure cooker in just two minutes. Asparagus is super healthy, but it's easy to under or overcook it. Luckily, the Instant Pot takes care of that, so you get perfectly-steamed veggies every time.

<u>Ingredients:</u>

1 lb. trimmed asparagus
1 cup of water
2 tablespoons olive oil
1 tablespoon of minced onion
Sea salt and pepper to taste
Squeeze of fresh lemon

<u>Directions:</u>

1. Pour water into your Instant Pot and lower in the steamer basket.
2. Put the asparagus in the basket.
3. Drizzle on a little olive oil and onion.
4. Close and seal the lid.
5. Select "steam" and adjust the time to 2 minutes.
6. When time is up, hit "cancel" and quick-release the pressure.
7. Serve with salt, pepper, and a squeeze of lemon juice.

Nutritional Info (¼ recipe):

Total calories: 84
Protein: 3
Carbs: 5
Fiber: 4
Fat: 0

Steamed Artichokes

Serves: 6

Time: 33 minutes (10 minutes prep time, 5 minutes cook time, 15 minutes dry time, 3 minutes fry time)

Artichokes are one of the healthiest veggies out there, but their intimidating hard bodies put a lot of people off. The prep is totally worth the result, especially when you can steam the artichokes to perfection in your pressure cooker. After cooking, you finish them off with a little frying in a separate skillet.

Ingredients:

6 long, narrow artichokes
3 smashed garlic cloves
2 cups water
1-2 cups of olive oil
Juice of 1 lemon
1 sliced lemon
1 tablespoon whole peppercorns

Directions:

1. Pour 2 cups of water, lemon juice, lemon slices, and peppercorns in your Instant Pot.
2. Prep artichokes by tearing off the tough leaves on the outside, peeling the stem, cutting off the end of the stem, and cutting the top half off of the leaves horizontally, so you end up with what looks like a hat.
3. Pry open the leaves and take out the hairy, hard part to access the heart, leaving the dotty part where the hairy part was attached.
4. Open the leaves up a bit more and dip in the pressure cooker, head down, and swirl around before putting in the steamer basket.
5. Put basket with artichokes in the pressure cooker.

6. Close and seal lid.
7. Select "manual" and cook on high pressure for 5 minutes.
8. When time is up, quick-release the pressure after hitting "cancel."
9. Shake the artichokes and put in a strainer for 15 minutes to dry out.
10. In a pan, heat up about 2 centimeters of oil and just fry the artichokes head down until their edges start to turn golden.
11. Plate and dab with a paper towel to remove excess oil before serving.

Nutritional Info (⅙ recipe):

Total calories: 40
Protein: 1
Carbs: 3
Fiber: 9
Fat: 2

Warm Caper + Beet Salad

<u>Serves</u>: 4-6

<u>Time</u>: 35 minutes (5 minutes prep time, 30 minutes cook time)

Fresh beets are a neglected vegetable, probably because people aren't sure how to cook them. In the pressure cooker, it's very easy, and these bright purple nutrition bombs go really well with ingredients like garlic, rice wine vinegar, and capers. It's nice to have a salad option that doesn't involve greens.

<u>Ingredients:</u>

4 medium-sized beets
1 cup water
2 tablespoons rice wine vinegar
1 garlic clove
2 tablespoons capers
1 tablespoon of chopped parsley
1 tablespoon olive oil
½ teaspoon salt
½ teaspoon black pepper

<u>Directions:</u>

1. Pour one cup of water into your Instant Pot and lower in the steamer basket.
2. Clean and trim the beets.
3. Put beets in the steamer basket.
4. Close and seal the lid.
5. Select "manual" and cook on high pressure for 25 minutes.
6. While that cooks, make the dressing by shaking chopped garlic, parsley, oil, salt, pepper, and capers in a jar.
7. When time is up, hit "cancel" and carefully quick-release the pressure.

8. Beets should be soft enough to pierce with a fork.
9. Run the beets under cold water and remove the skins.
10. Slice beets and serve with rice wine vinegar and jar dressing.

Nutritional Info (⅙ serving):

Total calories: 43.1
Protein: .7
Carbs: 5.4
Fiber: .8
Fat: 2.4

Classic Hummus (Oil Free)

<u>Serves</u>: 6-8

<u>Time</u>: 28 minutes (18 minutes cook time, 10 minutes natural release)

A traditional Middle Eastern spread, hummus can be expensive when you get it in the store, and there are always listeria recalls going on. That's not very delicious. Thankfully, you can make your own hummus in the Instant Pot very easily, and season it to your liking, whether you're a garlic lover and prefer it to be a bit more mild. Remember - you have to soak dry chickpeas overnight.

<u>Ingredients:</u>

6 cups water
1 cup soaked chickpeas
3-4 crushed garlic cloves
1 bay leaf
¼ cup chopped parsley
2 tablespoons tahini
1 juiced lemon
½ teaspoon salt
¼ teaspoon cumin
Dash of paprika

<u>Directions:</u>

1. Soak your chickpeas overnight in water.
2. When you're ready to make the hummus, rinse them and put them in the Instant Pot.
3. Pour in 6 cups of water.
4. Toss in the bay leaf and garlic cloves.
5. Close and seal the lid.
6. Select "manual," and cook for 18 minutes on high pressure.
7. When the beeper goes off, hit "cancel" and wait for the pressure to

come down on its own.

8. When the cooker is safe to open, drain the chickpeas, but save all the cooking liquid.
9. Remove the bay leaf before pureeing the chickpeas.
10. Add tahini, lemon juice, cumin, and ½ cup of cooking liquid to start.
11. Keep pureeing, and if the mixture isn't creamy enough, keep adding ½ cup of liquid at a time.
12. When it's the right level of creaminess, salt, and puree once more.
13. Serve with a sprinkle of paprika and fresh chopped parsley!

Nutritional Info (⅛ serving):

Total calories: 1o9
Protein: 4.1
Carbs: 3.5
Fiber: 3.3
Fat: 3.8

Chapter 10

Vegan Sauces

Tomato Sauce

<u>Makes</u>: 6 pounds
<u>Time</u>: 1 hour, 30 minutes (5 minutes prep time, 1 hour 25 minutes cook time)

Tomato sauce is one of those pantry essentials. While in theory, it should always be vegan-friendly, that doesn't mean it's always great. Making your own is much healthier, and with a pressure cooker, you can cook up to 6 pounds of plum tomatoes for a ton of sauce. It will last in your fridge for about 3 months.

<u>Ingredients:</u>

6 pounds quartered plum tomatoes
6-8 fresh basil leaves
2 big, chopped carrots
2-3 sliced, medium-sized yellow onions
4 tablespoons olive oil
1 chopped celery stalk

<u>Directions:</u>

1. Preheat your Instant Pot on "sauté."
2. Add oil and cook the sliced onions until soft.
3. Move the onions to the side, and add celery and carrots.
4. Cook and stir for 5 minutes or so.
5. Add tomatoes and mix.
6. Squish down the tomatoes, so they're below the "max" line of the pressure cooker, and they've released their juice.
7. When the pot reaches a boil, close and seal the lid.
8. Select "manual" and cook on high pressure for 5 minutes.
9. When the beeper sounds, hit "cancel" and carefully quick-release.
10. Turn the pot back to the lowest setting of "sauté," and cook for 1 hour.

11. Stir after 30 minutes, so nothing is sticking to the bottom.
12. After an hour, puree till smooth.
13. Pour sauce into 1-pint jars (putting one bay leaf at the bottom of the jar) and close.
14. Wait for the jars to cool before storing in the fridge.

Nutritional Info (¼ cup):

Total calories: 42.9
Protein: 1
Carbs: 6.1
Fiber: 1.5
Fat: 2.1

Zucchini Pesto

<u>Serves</u>: 4-6

<u>Time</u>: 13 minutes (10 minutes prep time, 3 minutes cook time)

If you ever find yourself overwhelmed with zucchini and don't know what to do with it, try this creamy zucchini pesto with garlic and basil. It only takes 3 minutes to cook in your Instant Pot, and goes great with pasta, as a sandwich spread, or mixed into salad dressing.

<u>Ingredients:</u>

1 ½ pounds chopped zucchini
1 chopped onion
¾ cup water
2 tablespoons olive oil
2 minced garlic cloves
1 bunch of basil (leaves picked off)
1 ½ teaspoons salt

<u>Directions:</u>

1. Prep your ingredients.
2. Preheat your Instant Pot before adding 1 tablespoon of oil and onion.
3. When soft, add the water, zucchini, and salt.
4. Close and seal the lid.
5. Select "manual" and cook for 3 minutes on high pressure.
6. When the timer beeps, turn off the cooker and quick-release the pressure.
7. Add garlic and basil leaves.
8. Puree the pesto until smooth.
9. For best results, serve right away with the last tablespoon of olive oil.

Nutritional Info (⅙ recipe):

Total calories: 71.4
Protein: 1.2
Carbs: 7.5
Fiber: 2.3
Fat: 4.7

Lentil Bolognese (Oil Free)

Serves: 4-6

Time: 30 minutes (5 minutes prep time, 15 minutes cook time, 10 minutes natural release)

Bolognese is traditionally a meaty tomato sauce, so for the vegan version, you replace meat with black lentils. These add a hearty texture, as well as tons of nutritional value. Ingredients like fire-roasted tomatoes, lots of garlic, and a little balsamic vinegar at the very end make the sauce taste like it's been simmering for hours, when in reality, the whole process only takes about a half hour.

Ingredients:

4 cups water
1 cup washed black lentils
1, 28-ounce can of fire-roasted tomatoes
4 minced garlic cloves
3 diced carrots
1 diced yellow onion
1 can tomato paste
¼ cup balsamic vinegar
2 tablespoons Italian seasoning
Red pepper flakes
Salt and pepper

Directions:

1. Add all your ingredients except the balsamic vinegar.
2. Stir.
3. Close and seal the lid.
4. Hit "manual" and adjust time to 15 minutes on high pressure.
5. When the beeper goes off, hit "cancel" and wait 10 minutes.
6. Quick-release any leftover pressure.

7. Add the balsamic vinegar, salt, and pepper and stir.
8. Serve or pour in a jar, that you let cool before storing in the fridge.

Nutritional Info (⅙ recipe):

Total calories: 208
Protein: 12
Carbs: 39
Fiber: 5
Fat: 0

Vegan "Cheese" Sauce (Oil Free)

<u>Serves</u>: 2-4 (depending on what you're using sauce for)
<u>Time</u>: 25 minutes (5 minutes prep time, 5 minutes cook time, 15 minutes cool time)

When you're making anything like cheese as a vegan, there are two key ingredients to pop up in just about every recipe: nutritional yeast and cashews. Nutritional yeast has a naturally-cheesy flavor, while cashews imitate the texture of cheese in cooking when they're blended. To make a "cheese" sauce you can use on just about anything, cook nutritional yeast and cashews in your Instant Pot, along with some potatoes, carrots, onion, and seasonings.

<u>Ingredients:</u>

2 cups peeled and chopped white potatoes
2 cups water
1 cup chopped carrots
3 peeled, whole garlic cloves
½ cup chopped onion
½ cup nutritional yeast
½ cup raw cashews
1 teaspoon turmeric
1 teaspoon salt

<u>Directions:</u>

1. Put everything in your Instant Pot.
2. Close and seal the lid.
3. Hit "manual" and cook for 5 minutes on high pressure.
4. When time is up, hit "cancel" and quick-release.
5. Let the sauce cool for 10-15 minutes.
6. Blend until smooth and creamy.
7. Serve or store!

Nutritional Info (¼ recipe):

Total calories: 216
Protein: 13
Carbs: 26
Fiber: 1.5
Fat: 9

Sage-Butternut Squash Sauce

Serves: 4

Time: 30 minutes (10 minutes prep time, 10 minutes cook time, 10 minutes natural release)

Cooked butternut squash is an excellent base for a sauce because of its easily-creamed texture. Fresh sage, crisped up in your pressure cooker before the squash, is a fantastic herb for squash. This sauce would be excellent during the winter.

Ingredients:

2 pounds chopped butternut squash
1 cup veggie broth
1 chopped yellow onion
2 chopped garlic cloves
2 tablespoons olive oil
1 tablespoon chopped sage
⅛ teaspoon red pepper flakes
Salt and black pepper to taste

Directions:

1. Preheat your cooker with oil.
2. Once the oil is hot, add the sage and stir so it becomes coated in oil.
3. When the sage crisps up, move it to a plate.
4. Add the onion to your cooker and cook until it begins to turn clear.
5. Add garlic and cook until fragrant.
6. Pour in 1 cup of broth and deglaze before adding squash.
7. Close and seal the lid.
8. Select "manual" and adjust time to 10 minutes.
9. When time is up, hit "cancel" and wait 10 minutes before releasing pressure.
10. When a little cooler, add the pot's contents (and the sage) to a

blender and puree till smooth.
11. If it's too thick, add a little more veggie broth.
12. Serve right away or store in the fridge no longer than 3-4 days.

Nutritional Info (¼ recipe):

Total calories: 179
Protein: 3
Carbs: 30
Fiber: 5
Fat: 7

Spicy Eggplant Sauce

<u>Serves</u>: 4-6

<u>Time</u>: 20 minutes (5 minutes prep time, 15 minutes cook time)

Earthy eggplant spiced with red pepper flakes makes for a great sauce. It's always nice to have sauce options that aren't tomato-based, but still have that satisfying richness. To make enough sauce, look for big eggplants, and plan on adding an extra half hour to the total time if you're going to follow the cooking tip about reducing bitterness.

Cooking Tip: If you find eggplant bitter, put the cubes in a strainer with some salt, and put a heavy plate on top of the cubes for at least a half hour. This will squeeze out the bitter juice.

<u>Ingredients:</u>

2 big, cubed eggplants
2 tablespoons olive oil
½ cup water
1 smashed garlic clove
1 tablespoon dry oregano
1-3 pinches of red pepper flakes
Sea salt to taste

<u>Directions:</u>

1. Prep your eggplants.
2. Sprinkle with a little salt.
3. Add oil, garlic, one pinch of pepper flakes, and oregano to your Instant Pot.
4. Turn the "keep warm" setting on and stir around for about 5 minutes.
5. If the oil starts to bubble, unplug the cooker.
6. Take out the garlic.

7. Brown half of the eggplant cubes in salt and pepper in your cooker on the "sauté" setting.
8. Add the rest of the eggplant and garlic.
9. Mix before pouring in water.
10. Close and seal the lid.
11. Select "manual" and cook on high pressure for 3 minutes.
12. Hit "cancel" when time is up, and quick-release the pressure.
13. Immediately remove the eggplant and cool for a few minutes.
14. Blend until smooth.
15. Add more red pepper flakes if you want the sauce spicier, and serve!

Nutritional Info (⅙ recipe):

Total calories: 79
Protein: 2
Carbs: 9
Fiber: 4.6
Fat: 5

Vegan Alfredo Sauce

Serves: 2-4

Time: 13 minutes (5 minutes prep time, 3 minutes cook time, 5 minutes natural pressure release)

Substituting cauliflower for dairy when you're making a cream sauce produces a very similar texture, and when seasoned right, a similar taste. Cauliflower cooks very quickly in a pressure cooker, so you can have a fresh sauce in just over 10 minutes.

Cooking Tip: If you want a "cheesier" taste to your sauce, add nutritional yeast.

Ingredients:

12-ounces cauliflower florets
2 minced garlic cloves
½ cup water
1 teaspoon coconut oil
½ teaspoon sea salt
Black pepper to taste

Directions:

1. Heat the oil in your Instant Pot and add garlic.
2. When the garlic has become fragrant, pour ½ cup water into the pressure cooker.
3. Pour cauliflower in your steamer basket, and lower into the cooker.
4. Close and seal the lid.
5. Select "manual" and cook for 3 minutes on high pressure.
6. When time is up, hit "cancel" and wait for the pressure to come down on its own.
7. The cauliflower should be very soft.
8. When a little cooler, add cauliflower and cooking liquid to a blender

and process until smooth.
9.   Season with salt and pepper before serving with pasta.

Nutritional Info (¼ recipe):

Total calories: 19
Protein: 1
Carbs: 2
Fiber: 1.7
Fat: 1

Carrot-Tomato Sauce

<u>Makes</u>: 3 cups

<u>Time</u>: 45 minutes (5 minutes prep time, 15 minutes cook time, 15 minutes natural release, 10 minutes simmer)

This unique take on tomato sauce is basically a combination of a traditional spaghetti sauce and a cashew-based cream sauce. Tomatoes and carrots are both naturally sweet, and the pressure cooker really brings out their flavors. The cashews, soaked for 2-3 hours and added at the very end, turn up the creaminess. Be sure to season with plenty of garlic and salt.

<u>Ingredients:</u>

9-10 medium-sized, quartered tomatoes
8 medium-sized, diced carrots
8 minced garlic cloves
½ chopped white onion
½ cup soaked cashews
¼ cup water
1 tablespoon olive oil

<u>Directions:</u>

1. Heat oil in your Instant Pot and add garlic.
2. When fragrant, add onions and stir for 1-2 minutes.
3. Add carrots and tomatoes.
4. Cook for another few minutes.
5. Pour in water and stir.
6. Close and seal the lid.
7. Select "manual" and cook on LOW pressure for 15 minutes.
8. When time is up, hit "cancel" and wait for a natural pressure release.
9. The veggies should be extremely soft, because you're going to puree them.
10. Move to a blender and puree.

11. Pour the sauce back into the cooker, leaving 1 cup in the blender.
12. Add your soaked cashews to the blender and puree.
13. Pour back into the pot and simmer without the lid for 10 minutes, until thickened.
14. Season to taste.

Nutritional Info (1 cup):

Total calories: 284
Protein: 10
Carbs: 35
Fiber: 11
Fat: 14

Mixed-Veggie Sauce

Serves: 3

Time: 26 minutes (10 minutes prep time, 6 minutes cook time, 10 minutes natural release)

This sauce is packed with veggies - from pumpkin to carrots. The flavor result is bright, a little sweet, and a little spicy. Serve with pasta or over more veggies!

Ingredients:

4 chopped tomatoes
4-5 cubes of pumpkin
4 minced garlic cloves
2 chopped green chilies
2 chopped celery stalks
1 sliced leek
1 chopped onion
1 chopped red bell pepper
1 chopped carrot
1 tablespoon sugar
2 teaspoons olive oil
1 teaspoon red chili flakes
Splash of vinegar
Salt to taste

Directions:

1. Prep your veggies.
2. Heat your oil in the Instant Pot.
3. Add onion and garlic, and cook until the onion is clear.
4. Add pumpkin, carrots, green chilies, and bell pepper.
5. Stir before adding the leek, celery, and tomatoes.
6. After a minute or so, toss in salt and red chili flakes.

7. Close and seal the pressure cooker.
8. Adjust time to 6 minutes on the "manual" setting.
9. When time is up, hit "cancel" and let the pressure come down on its own.
10. The veggies should be very soft.
11. Let the mixture cool a little before moving to a blender.
12. Puree until smooth.
13. Pour back into the pot and add vinegar and sugar.
14. Simmer on the lowest sauté setting for a few minutes before serving.

Nutritional Info (⅓ recipe):

Total calories: 126
Protein: 3
Carbs: 22
Fiber: 4
Fat: 3

Homemade Ketchup

<u>Makes</u>: 3 cups

<u>Time</u>: 30 minutes (5 minutes prep time, 5 minutes cook time, 10 minutes natural pressure release, 10 minutes simmer)

Ketchup is one of those condiments most people use a lot. Once you taste the homemade version, you'll wonder why you ever used store-bought. The flavors are fresher, richer, and it has much less sugar. It lasts in the fridge for about 6 months.

<u>Ingredients:</u>

2 pounds quartered plum tomatoes
1 tablespoon paprika
1 tablespoon agave syrup
1 teaspoon salt
6 tablespoons apple cider vinegar
⅓ cup raisins
⅛ wedged onion
½ teaspoon dijon mustard
¼ teaspoon celery seeds
⅛ teaspoon garlic powder
⅛ teaspoon ground clove
⅛ teaspoon cinnamon

<u>Directions:</u>

1. Put everything in the Instant Pot.
2. Mash down so the tomatoes release their juice, making sure you hit the 1 ½ cups minimum for the cooker.
3. Close and seal the lid.
4. Select "manual" and cook for 5 minutes on high pressure.
5. When the beeper goes off, hit "cancel" and wait for a natural pressure release.

6. Take the lid off and simmer for 10 minutes to reduce.
7. Puree in a blender before storing in a jar.
8. Wait until it's cooled down before putting in the fridge.

Nutritional Info (1 tablespoon):

Total calories: 6.8
Protein: .1
Carbs: 1.7
Fiber: .2
Fat: .1

Chapter 11

Holiday Foods

Vegan Holiday Roast with Mashed Vegetables

Serves: 4-6
Time: 10 minutes (2 minutes prep time, 8 minutes cook time)

Holidays can be a tough time for vegans, but you can make an awesome dinner that everyone - vegan or not - will love. In this recipe, you make roast right in the instant pot with veggies for mashing at the same time. You can buy stuffed vegan roasts from brands like Field Roast.

Ingredients:

1, 1 lb. (thawed) vegan stuffed roast
2 cups diced potato
2 cups diced carrots
1 cup diced yellow onion
¾-1 cup of veggie broth
4 minced garlic cloves
1 tablespoon almond milk
1 teaspoon olive oil
Salt and pepper to taste

Directions:

1.   Heat the oil in your Instant Pot.
2.   When hot, cook garlic and onion for 1 minute.
3.   Add carrots, potatoes, and salt, and mix.
4.   Put the roast on top of the veggies, and pour over the broth.
5.   Close and seal the lid.
6.   Select "manual" and cook on low pressure for 8 minutes, or high pressure for about 6 minutes.
7.   When time is up, hit "cancel" and quick-release.
8.   Take out the roast.
9.   Add almond milk and pepper to the veggies, and mash to your

desired consistency.
10. Serve!

Nutritional Info (⅙ recipe):

Total calories: 246
Protein: 19
Carbs: 22
Fiber: 3
Fat: 9

Mashed Potatoes with Pine Nuts

Serves: 6
Time: 25 minutes (10 minutes prep time, 15 minutes cook time)

Mashed potatoes are a family favorite during the holiday season, but with all that cream and butter, how can vegans enjoy it? Easy! Just use soy milk and Earth Balance butter, or another vegan butter. Pureed pine nuts also help add creaminess, as well as a lovely mild nutty flavor.

Ingredients:

4 pounds peeled and rinsed potatoes
1 ½ cups water + ½ cup
⅛ cup pine nuts
2 tablespoons olive-oil Earth Balance
1 teaspoon salt
Unsweetened soy milk

Directions:

1. Pour 1 ½ cups water in your Instant Pot.
2. Lower in the steamer basket with the potatoes.
3. Close and seal the lid.
4. Hit "steam," and cook for 15 minutes.
5. In the meanwhile, blend ½ cup water with the pine nuts.
6. When the pressure cooker beeps, hit "cancel" and quick-release.
7. Carefully take out the potatoes and poke with a knife.
8. Mash potatoes in a blender with ¼ cup soy milk, the pine nut mixture, Earth Balance, and salt. Add soy milk as needed in ¼ cup increments.
9. Enjoy!

Nutritional Info (⅙ recipe):

Total calories: 325
Protein: 8
Carbs: 60
Fiber: 5
Fat: 6

Cranberry Sauce (Oil Free)

<u>Makes</u>: 1 cup
<u>Time</u>: 18 minutes (3 minutes cook time, 5 minutes simmer time, 10 minutes rest time)

Homemade cranberry sauce can be a real pain to make, but this recipe uses dried cranberries that are reconstituted in your Instant Pot. If you're making sauce for a lot of people, you can double the recipe, but since you can only fill your cooker ½-way full, you should make the sauce in batches if you want more than 2 cups. Once in the fridge, the sauce will last up to a week.

<u>Ingredients</u>:

1 cup dried cranberries
¾ cup water
¾ cup cranberry juice cocktail
1 teaspoon fresh lemon juice

<u>Directions</u>:

1. Put all the ingredients in your Instant Pot.
2. Close and seal the lid.
3. Press "manual" and adjust time to 3 minutes.
4. When the beeper goes off, very slowly release the pressure through the valve.
5. Pour sauce into a blender (or use a hand blender) to break up the berries, but don't puree entirely.
6. Simmer in the pot without the lid for 5 minutes while stirring to get the texture you want.
7. Turn off the heat and let the sauce rest for 10 minutes.
8. Serve right away, or chill in the fridge.

Nutritional Info (3 teaspoons):

Total calories: 30.1
Protein: 0
Carbs: 7.9
Fiber: .4
Fat: .1

Dried-Fruit Wild Rice

Serves: 6-8

Time: 50 minutes (30 minutes cook time, 20 minutes natural release)

Wild rice pairs really well with cranberries and other dried fruit for an earthy, rustic holiday dish. It would also work really well as a stuffing or dressing. It's on the sweet side, but the black pepper helps offset that.

Cooking Tip: You can eat this rice as-is, or for a full meal, you can fill a partially-baked butternut squash with the rice and bake for 30-45 minutes in a 350-degree oven.

Ingredients:

3 ½ cups water
1 ½ cups wild rice
1 cup dried, mixed fruit
2 peeled and chopped small apples
1 chopped pear
½ cup slivered almonds
2 tablespoons apple juice
1 tablespoon maple syrup
1 teaspoon veggie oil
1 teaspoon cinnamon
½ teaspoon ground nutmeg
Salt and pepper to taste

Directions:

1. Pour water into your Instant Pot along the rice.
2. Close and seal the lid.
3. Select "manual," and cook for 30 minutes on high pressure.
4. While that cooks, soak the dried fruit in just enough apple juice to cover everything.

5. After 30 minutes, drain the fruit.
6. By now, the rice should be done, so hit "cancel" and wait for the pressure to come down on its own.
7. Drain the rice and move rice to a bowl.
8. Turn your pressure cooker to sauté and add veggie oil.
9. Cook the apples, pears, and almonds for about 2 minutes.
10. Pour in two tablespoons apple juice and keep cooking for a few minutes more.
11. Add syrup, the cooked rice, soaked fruit, and seasonings.
12. Keep stirring for 2-3 minutes.
13. Serve!

Nutritional Info (⅛ recipe):

Total calories: 226
Protein: 6
Carbs: 43
Fiber: 5.6
Fat: 3

Stewed Tomatoes + Green Beans

<u>Serves</u>: 4-6

<u>Time</u>: 10 minutes (5 minutes prep time, 5 minutes cook time)

This simple and healthy side dish pairs tomatoes with green beans and garlic, resulting in bright and fresh flavors. You can use frozen green beans and canned tomatoes if you have to, though in my opinion, fresh is always better, if it's the season for it.

<u>Ingredients:</u>

1 pound trimmed green beans
2 cups fresh, chopped tomatoes
1 crushed garlic clove
1 teaspoon olive oil
Salt

<u>Directions:</u>

1. Preheat your Instant Pot.
2. When warm, add 1 teaspoon of olive oil and garlic.
3. When the garlic has become fragrant and golden, add tomatoes and stir.
4. If the tomatoes are dry, add ½ cup water.
5. Fill the steamer basket with the green beans and sprinkle on salt.
6. Lower into cooker.
7. Close and seal the lid.
8. Select "manual," and cook for 5 minutes on high pressure.
9. When the timer beeps, turn off cooker and quick-release.
10. Carefully remove the steamer basket and pour beans into the tomato sauce.
11. If the beans aren't quite tender enough, simmer in sauce for a few minutes.
12. Serve!

Nutritional Info (⅙ recipe):

Total calories: 55.3
Protein: 1.6
Carbs: 6.3
Fiber: 2.6
Fat: 3.2

Brussels Sprouts with Pine Nuts and Pomegranate

Serves: 4-6

Time: 13 minutes (10 minutes prep time, 3 minutes cook time)

When winter comes along, so do the Brussels sprouts. On their own, they're a little bland, so to dress things up, add toasted pine nuts and sour-sweet pomegranates. There are layers of texture *and* flavor going on in this side dish, and you only use a total of six ingredients counting salt and pepper.

Ingredients:

1 pound Brussels sprouts
Seeds of 1 pomegranate
¼ cup toasted pine nuts
Olive oil
Salt and pepper to taste

Directions:

1. Peel off the outer leaves of your sprouts and trim the stems.
2. Wash.
3. Cut any especially big ones in half before putting in the steamer basket.
4. Pour 1 cup of water into your Instant Pot.
5. Lower in the steamer basket.
6. Close and seal the lid.
7. Click "manual" and adjust time to 3 minutes.
8. When the timer beeps, hit "cancel" and quick-release.
9. Drain the sprouts.

10. Pour into a bowl and add toasted pine nuts and pomegranate seeds.
11. Drizzle on a little olive oil and season.
12. Serve!

Nutritional Info (⅙ recipe):

Total calories: 115
Protein: 5
Carbs: 16
Fiber: 4.6
Fat: 6

Citrus Cauliflower Salad

<u>Serves:</u> 4
<u>Time:</u> 16 minutes (10 minutes prep time, 6 minutes cook time)

A lot of side dishes can be too hearty and filling. The other option is a salad, but it's easy for those to get really old. For something a bit different, try this cauliflower-and-broccoli mix with a spicy orange vinaigrette.

Ingredients:

Florets from 1 small cauliflower
Florets from 1 small Romanesco cauliflower
1 pound broccoli
2 peeled and sliced seedless oranges

1 zested and squeezed orange
1 sliced hot pepper
4 tablespoons olive oil
1 tablespoon capers (not rinsed)
Salt to taste
Pepper to taste

Directions:

1. Pour 1 cup of water into your Instant Pot.
2. Add florets into your steamer basket and lower in the cooker.
3. Close and seal.
4. Hit "steam" and cook for 6 minutes.
5. While that cooks, make your vinaigrette.
6. Mix the orange juice, zest, hot pepper, capers, olive oil, salt, and pepper.
7. Peel your oranges and slice very thin.
8. When the timer beeps, hit "cancel" and quick-release.
9. Mix florets with oranges and dress with the vinaigrette.

Nutritional Info (¼ recipe):

Total calories: 241
Protein: 3
Carbs: 22
Fiber: 8
Fat: 15

Thanksgiving Stuffing (Oil Free)

Serves: 6

Time: 35 minutes (10 minutes prep time, 15 minutes cook time, 10 minutes oven time)

Not only is this stuffing vegan, it's gluten free. You use a mixture of almond meal, almond milk, and fresh herbs instead of breadcrumbs. The stuffing itself is a nutritious (and delicious) mix of carrots, onions, eggplant, apple, and more. After cooking in the pressure cooker, you finish everything off in the oven to give the stuffing a classic crispy texture.

Ingredients:

2-3 chopped carrots
3 chopped spring onions
2 chopped celery stalks
1 cubed eggplant
1 chopped fennel bulb
1 chopped apple
1 cup almond meal
½ cup almond milk + 1 tablespoon almond milk
1 tablespoon chopped fresh herbs
Salt and pepper to taste

Directions:

1. Mix almond meal, 1 tablespoon almond milk, and herbs in a bowl and mix with your fingers until it becomes crumbly.
2. Mix the rest of your ingredients in a dish you know fits in the Instant Pot, with ½ cup of almond milk poured on top.
3. Stir.
4. Pour 1 cup of water into your pressure cooker and put the dish inside, on top of a trivet.
5. Close and seal the lid.

6. Select "manual" and cook on high pressure for 15 minutes.
7. When time is up, hit "cancel" and quick-release the pressure.
8. Pour stuffing on a greased, foil-lined cookie sheet and mix with the almond meal crumble.
9. Cook for 10 minutes in a 350-degree oven so stuffing gets crispy.

Nutritional Info (⅙ recipe):

Total calories: 195
Protein: 7
Carbs: 19
Fiber: 4.3
Fat: 11

Maple Syrup-Sweetened Cornbread

<u>Makes</u>: 12-16 squares

<u>Time</u>: 54 minutes (2 minutes prep time, 22 minutes cook time, 30 minutes natural release/cool time)

This cornbread is not too sweet, so it can be served with jam or something savory, like smashed avocado or holiday stuffing. To make it, it's a simple process of mixing liquid ingredients, then dry, and then mixing them together. A Bundt pan is a good choice, and it gives the cornbread a pretty shape for the table.

<u>Ingredients:</u>

2 cups cornmeal
2 cups soy milk
1 cup flour
⅓ cup veggie oil
2 tablespoons maple syrup
2 teaspoons baking powder
2 teaspoons apple cider vinegar
½ teaspoon salt

<u>Directions:</u>

1. In a bowl, mix soy milk and apple cider vinegar together.
2. In another bowl, mix dry ingredients.
3. Add veggie oil and maple syrup to your soy milk/vinegar mixture.
4. Whisk until it's foaming, which should be about 2 minutes.
5. Pour the wet into the dry, mixing with a wooden spoon.
6. Pour into a greased Bundt pan.
7. Prepare your Instant Pot with ⅔ cup of water and seal the lid.
8. Adjust time to 22 minutes after hitting "manual."
9. When time is up, hit "cancel" and wait for a natural release.
10. When the pressure is gone, take out the pan and let cool before

taking out the bread.

Nutritional Info (1 square):

Total calories: 212
Protein: 5
Carbs: 33
Fiber: 2.7
Fat: 7

Personal Vegetable Pot Pies (Oil Free)

<u>Serves</u>: 5

<u>Time</u>: 18 minutes (15 minutes prep time, 3 minutes cook time)

Pot pies are one of the best comfort foods. A flaky biscuit top hides a hot, flavorful filling packed with veggies and seasonings. For this recipe, you make individual pot pies, so everyone gets a whole biscuit to themselves.

Cooking Tip: If you don't want to bother washing your pressure cooker in the middle of the recipe, cook your sauce in a separate skillet.

<u>Ingredients:</u>

5 raw biscuits
2 cups veggie broth
2 cups mixed, frozen veggies
2 bay leaves
1 minced garlic clove
½ medium yellow onion
¼ cup unsweetened almond milk
¼ cup flour
Salt and pepper to taste

<u>Directions:</u>

1. Turn on your Instant Pot to sauté and add onion and garlic.
2. Cook until they've softened.
3. Add flour and whisk quickly before gradually adding broth, whisking as you go.
4. Pour in the almond milk and toss in bay leaves.
5. Simmer for 10 minutes until thickened.
6. Grease 5 ramekins.

7. When your pot-pie sauce is thickened, add frozen veggies and cook for 5 minutes more.
8. Add salt and pepper.
9. Pick out the bay leaves.
10. Pour sauce evenly into your ramekins.
11. Now, you'll need to clean your pressure cooker.
12. When it's clean, pour in 1 cup of water.
13. Put one raw biscuit on top of each ramekin and loosely wrap in foil, covering top, but not too tightly because biscuit will rise slightly.
14. Put ramekins in steamer basket.
15. Lower into cooker.
16. Select "manual" and adjust time to 3 minutes on high pressure.
17. When time is up, hit "cancel" and quick-release.
18. Cool for a little before serving!

Nutritional Info (⅕ recipe):

Total calories: 307
Protein: 8.3
Carbs: 41
Fiber: 4.7
Fat: 12

Corn Chowder

<u>Serves</u>: 6

<u>Time</u>: 31 minutes (10 minutes prep time, 6 minutes cook time, 15 minutes natural release)

Corn chowder really brings out the awesome flavors of corn - the sweetness and hint of nuttiness. Try this out when corn is in season at family gatherings, and if you think it's too hot for chowder, you can actually serve it chilled for a refreshing take on the classic.

Cooking Tip: If you want to use fresh corn, you'll need 5 ears, and you actually put the cobs in the pressure cooker before you bring it to pressure, giving the chowder a really true flavor.

<u>Ingredients:</u>

4 cups veggie broth
3 ½ cups of corn
1 cup coconut milk
3 minced garlic cloves
3 big chopped carrots
3 chopped Yukon Gold potatoes
1 tablespoon coconut oil
1 diced onion
1 tablespoon potato starch
Juice of 1 lime
1 teaspoon smoked paprika
1 teaspoon salt
1 teaspoon black pepper
½ teaspoon cumin
⅛ teaspoon crushed red pepper flakes

Directions:

1. Preheat your Instant Pot.
2. Add oil.
3. Cook carrots, onion, corn, and red pepper flakes until the carrots begin to turn clear.
4. Add garlic and cook for 1 minute.
5. Pour in broth, along with potatoes, salt, and pepper.
6. Hit "manual," and adjust time to 6 minutes.
7. When time is up, hit "cancel" and wait 15 minutes for the pressure to come down.
8. In a small bowl, mix coconut milk with potato starch until smooth.
9. Add lime juice before pouring into the pot.
10. Turn your cooker back to "sauté" to activate the thickening process.
11. With a hand blender, process until smooth. If you need to use a regular blender, puree the chowder *before* you add the coconut milk/starch/lime mixture.
12. Season to taste if necessary. Serve hot or chilled.

Nutritional Info (⅙ recipe):

Total calories: 266
Protein: 5
Carbs: 38
Fiber: 5
Fat: 11

Sweet Potato Casserole

<u>Serves</u>: 4
<u>Time</u>: 45 minutes (15 minutes cook time, 10 minutes natural release, 20 minutes oven time)

The longest part of this classic dish is cooking the sweet potatoes. With the Instant Pot, it comes significantly shorter, and ensures all the vitamin A, vitamin C, and antioxidants are all preserved. After mashing the potatoes with a mixture of vegan oils, syrup, and spices, and topping it with sweetened pecans and oats, you bake the dish in an oven to finish it off.

<u>Ingredients:</u>

2 ¼ cups sweet potatoes
1 ¼ tablespoons pure maple syrup
¾ tablespoons vegan butter
¾ tablespoons coconut oil
½ teaspoon pure vanilla
Sprinkle of cinnamon
Sprinkle of ground nutmeg
Salt to taste

½ cup rolled oats
½ cup chopped pecan halves
1 tablespoon melted vegan butter
1 tablespoon melted coconut oil
1 tablespoon pure maple syrup
⅙ cup almond flour
½ teaspoon cinnamon
Sprinkle of salt

<u>Directions:</u>

1. Chop sweet potatoes and put into steamer basket.

2. Pour in 1 cup of water.
3. Close and lock lid.
4. Select "manual," and adjust time to 15 minutes on high pressure.
5. When time is up, use a natural release for 10 minutes, and then quick-release.
6. Potatoes should be fork-tender.
7. While that potatoes cook, pulse the oats a few times.
8. Mix with the chopped pecans, almond meal, salt, and cinnamon.
9. Pour the melted butter and oil over the oats, adding maple syrup, and stir.
10. Drain the potatoes, if you haven't already.
11. Put in a bowl, and mash well with ¾ tablespoons of (melted) oil and butter until smooth and creamy.
12. Still looking to the first ingredient list, add maple syrup, cinnamon, nutmeg, salt, and vanilla.
13. Pour into a baking dish and smooth with a spatula.
14. Sprinkle on the oat topping.
15. Bake in a 375-degree oven for 20 minutes or so, until the dish is heated through and the topping is crispy.
16. Serve!

Nutritional Info (¼ recipe):

Total calories: 433
Protein: 6
Carbs: 48
Fiber: 4.5
Fat: 26

Chapter 12

Sips and Syrups

Pressure-Cooker Chai Tea

Makes: 1 ½ cups
Time: 3 minutes

Chai tea is a spicy, rich treat that's a great alternative to coffee. This recipe makes 1 ½ cups, but you can make a bigger batch if you want. The key is to cook the tea on low pressure - high pressure is too strong for delicate tea, and it will taste bitter. Also, be sure to go easy on the ginger, or it curdles your milk.

Ingredients:

1 cup water + ½ cup water
1 cup almond milk
1 ½ teaspoons black loose-leaf tea powder
2 crushed cardamom pods
2 crushed cloves
2 teaspoons sugar
1 teaspoon crushed ginger

Directions:

1. Pour 1 cup of water into your Instant Pot.
2. Put a bowl in the cooker on top of a trivet, and add all the ingredients.
3. Close and seal cooker.
4. Hit "manual" and cook on low pressure for 3 minutes.
5. When time is up, hit "cancel" and quick-release.
6. Strain the tea into a favorite mug, and enjoy!

Nutritional Info (1 recipe):

Total calories: 93
Protein: 1
Carbs: 10
Fiber: 0
Fat: 4

Vanilla-Ginger Syrup

<u>Makes</u>: 2 cups
<u>Time</u>: 45 minutes (25 minutes cook time, 20 minutes natural release)

This syrup is perfect for making boozy drinks and sodas. It's beautifully fragrant and not too sweet, like store-bought syrups. It would also be a tasty dressing for fresh fruit salad.

<u>Ingredients:</u>

2 cups water
2 cups sugar
1 split vanilla bean
8-ounce thumb of fresh ginger
Pinch of salt

<u>Directions:</u>

1. Rinse the ginger before slicing, and then chopping up.
2. Pour water, chopped ginger, salt, sugar, and vanilla bean into the Instant Pot.
3. Close and seal the pressure cooker.
4. Hit "manual," and cook for 25 minutes on high pressure.
5. When time is up, hit "cancel" and let the pressure come down on its own.
6. Pour through a strainer into a glass container.
7. Store in the fridge for up to 3 weeks.

Nutritional Info (1 tablespoon):

Total calories: 104
Protein: 0
Carbs: 26
Fiber: 0
Fat: 0

Elderberry Syrup

<u>Makes</u>: 1 quart

<u>Time</u>: 20 minutes (10 minutes cook time, 10 minutes natural release)

Tired of regular syrup? Elderberry syrup is fruity, sweet, and perfect for waffles, pancakes, and more. Research has shown that elderberries have powerful health benefits, so it can also help cut illnesses short.

<u>Ingredients</u>:

4 cups water
1 cup dried elderberries
¾-1 cup agave syrup
1 split vanilla bean

<u>Directions</u>:

1. Put all your ingredients (minus the agave) in the Instant Pot and stir well.
2. Close and seal the lid.
3. Select "manual," and cook on high pressure for just 10 minutes.
4. When time is up, hit "cancel" and wait for a natural release.
5. Pour syrup into a fine-mesh strainer and throw away elderberries. You will have to press down on the berries to get all the juice out.
6. Let the syrup cool before whisking in agave.
7. Store in a fridge for up to 2 weeks, or freeze to make it last longer.

<u>Nutritional Info (1 tablespoon)</u>:

Total calories: 25
Protein: 0
Carbs: 6
Fiber: 0
Fat: 0

Blackberry Soda Syrup

<u>Makes</u>: About 1 cup
<u>Time</u>: 30 minutes (15 minutes cook time, 10 minutes natural release, 5 minutes stovetop time)

To make sparkling Italian sodas, you need fruit syrups. This recipe is for blackberry syrup, which produces a sophisticated, unique drink that people will rave about.

<u>Ingredients:</u>

14-ounces washed and dried blackberries
2 cups white sugar
1 cup water

<u>Directions:</u>

1. Pour one cup of water into your Instant Pot.
2. Pour berries into your steamer basket and lower into the cooker.
3. Close and seal lid.
4. Select "manual" and cook on high pressure for 15 minutes.
5. When time is up, hit "cancel" and wait for pressure to come down.
6. Take out the steamer basket.
7. Pour juice-infused water into a measuring cup. Take note of how much it is.
8. Pour this cup into a saucepan and add twice the amount of sugar as there is juice-water.
9. On medium heat, stir the pot until sugar is fully dissolved.
10. Store in your fridge for 1-2 months.

Nutritional Info (1 tablespoon):

Total calories: 167
Protein: 0
Carbs: 46
Fiber: 0
Fat: 0

Peach Simple Syrup

Makes: About 1 cup
Time: 55 minutes (5 minutes cook time, 10 minutes natural release time, 30-40 minutes boil time)

Simple syrup is a key ingredient in cocktails. A homemade jar is also a fantastic hostess gift. Measurements are a bit up in the air - the key is to never fill your pressure cooker more than halfway full with fruit and water, and when you start to boil your mixture, you want to add twice as much sugar as there is fruit extract, so always measure your fruit extract before adding sugar.

Ingredients:

4 cups fresh, chopped peaches
2 cups water
2 cups sugar

Directions:

1. Pour peaches into your Instant Pot with water. Make sure it is no more than halfway full.
2. Close and seal the lid.
3. Select "manual" and cook on high pressure for 5 minutes.
4. When time is up, hit "cancel" and wait for the pressure to descend naturally.
5. Mash peaches before moving to a strainer.
6. Strain pot contents back into the pressure cooker.
7. On the sauté setting, bring to a boil, adding sugar, and boil until liquid has reduced in half.
8. Cool before pouring into glass jars.
9. Store in fridge and use for up to 2 weeks.

Nutritional Info (1 tablespoon):

Total calories: 97
Protein: 0
Carbs: 28
Fiber: 0
Fat: 0

Cranberry Simple Syrup

<u>Makes</u>: About 1 cup
<u>Time</u>: 55 minutes (5 minutes cook time, 10 minutes natural release time, 30-40 minutes boil time)

This recipe is basically the same as the peach simple syrup, except you're using dried cranberries. When you use dried fruit, you always use half the amount you would use for fresh fruit.

<u>Ingredients:</u>

2 cups dried cranberries
2 cups water
2 cups sugar

<u>Directions:</u>

1. Pour water into your Instant Pot along with the fruit. Be sure it is no more than halfway full, or you'll have to reduce your measurements.
2. Close and seal the lid.
3. Select "manual" and adjust time to 5 minutes on high pressure.
4. When the beeper sounds, hit "cancel" and wait for pressure to descend naturally.
5. Pour pot contents into a fine-mesh strainer (with a bowl to catch everything) and press down on fruit to get all the juice out.
6. Pour pot contents back into the pressure cooker.
7. On the sauté setting, add sugar.
8. Bring to a boil and let it roll until liquid has reduced in half.
9. Cool completely before pouring into glass jars.
10. Store in fridge and use for up to 2 weeks.

Nutritional Info (1 tablespoon):

Total calories: 130
Protein: 0
Carbs: 38
Fiber: 0
Fat: 0

Wassail (Hot Mulled Cider)

<u>Makes</u>: 12 cups
<u>Time</u>: 20 minutes (10 minutes cook time, 10 minutes natural release)

Wassail is hot mulled cider. It's an awesome non-alcoholic drink brimming with spices like clove, vanilla, and ginger. It's perfect for parties, and will make your home smell amazing.

<u>Ingredients:</u>

8 cups apple cider
4 cups orange juice
10 cloves
2 split vanilla beans
5 cinnamon sticks
1-inch piece of peeled ginger
Juice and zest of two lemons
½ teaspoon nutmeg

<u>Directions:</u>

1. Pour juice and cider into your Instant Pot.
2. Add the lemon, cinnamon, cloves, nutmeg, ginger, and vanilla beans in your steamer basket, and lower into cooker.
3. Close and seal lid.
4. Hit "manual," and cook on high for 10 minutes.
5. When time is up, hit "cancel" and let the pressure come down naturally.
6. Take out the steamer basket and throw away stuff.
7. To keep the drink hot, use the "keep warm" setting.

Nutritional Info (1 cup):

Total calories: 83
Protein: 1
Carbs: 9
Fiber: 0
Fat: 0

Homemade Ginger-Lemon Cough Syrup

<u>Makes</u>: 2 cups
<u>Time</u>: 20 minutes

For an all-natural cough syrup, you just simmer ginger and thyme in water, and add in vegan-friendly honey, lemon juice, and pepper at the end. When you have a bad cough, take 1 tablespoon to soothe your throat, and boost your immune system.

<u>Ingredients:</u>

2 cups water
1 cup vegan honey
8 sprigs fresh thyme
¼ cup chopped ginger
Juice of 1 lemon
⅛ teaspoon cayenne pepper

<u>Directions:</u>

1. Pour water in your Instant Pot, adding the ginger and thyme.
2. Hit "sauté" and simmer until the water has reduced in half.
3. Turn off the cooker and wait until the liquid is warm, not hot.
4. Strain the herbs out, saving the infused water.
5. Pour water back into the pressure cooker.
6. Add lemon, honey, and pepper.
7. Pour into a jar.
8. Store in the cupboard for 1 week, and if there's still syrup left, move to the fridge.

Nutritional Info (1 tablespoon):

Total calories: 31
Protein: 0
Carbs: 8
Fiber: 0
Fat: 0

Peppermint Crio Bru (Oil Free)

<u>Serves</u>: 8
<u>Time</u>: 15 minutes (5 minutes cook time, 10 minutes natural release)

Crio Bru is a brand that sells 100% cacao beans that are roasted and ground. It comes in peppermint flavor, and that provides the base for this homemade hot drink that tastes like Christmas in a cup.

<u>Ingredients:</u>

6 cups water
2 cups unsweetened vanilla almond milk
½ cup Crio Bru ground cocoa beans (peppermint flavor)
⅓ cup agave syrup
1 teaspoon pure vanilla
1 teaspoon peppermint extract

<u>Directions:</u>

1. Put beans, water, milk, puree, cinnamon, vanilla, and syrup in your Instant Pot.
2. Close and seal lid.
3. On the "manual" setting, adjust time to 5 minutes on high pressure.
4. When time is up, hit "cancel" and wait 10 minutes before quick-releasing.
5. Pour drink through a fine-mesh strainer to filter out grounds.
6. Serve hot or chilled.

Nutritional Info (⅛ recipe):

Total calories: 59
Protein: 3
Carbs: 14
Fiber: 0
Fat: 3

Homemade Vanilla Extract

<u>Makes</u>: 1 pint
<u>Time</u>: 45 minutes, 1 night (30 minutes cook time, 15 minutes natural release, overnight cool time)

Vanilla extract is a kitchen staple. Did you know you can make it yourself extremely easily right in the pressure cooker? The better beans you get, the better your extract will be. It only takes about 45 minutes to make, but you have to cool it overnight before use.

<u>Ingredients:</u>

2 cups 40% alcohol vodka
6-10 Madagascar vanilla beans

<u>Directions:</u>

1. Slice the vanilla beans in half.
2. Put the vanilla beans in a pint jar and pour in vodka, leaving 1-inch of space on top.
3. Put the ring and lid on, but only tighten a little.
4. Pour 1 cup of water into your Instant Pot and lower in trivet.
5. Put the jar in the cooker.
6. Close and seal the lid.
7. Hit "manual" and cook on high pressure for 30 minutes.
8. When time is up, hit "cancel" and wait for a natural release.
9. Take out the jar, carefully, and cool overnight.
10. When cool, store in a cupboard.

<u>Nutritional Info (1 tablespoon):</u>

Total calories: 12
Protein: 0
Carbs: 1
Fiber: 0
Fat: 0

Chapter 13

Desserts

Tapioca Pudding (Oil Free)

Serves: 4-6

Time: 28 minutes (8 minutes cook time, 20 minutes natural release time)

Tapioca pudding is a classic comfort dessert and one of the foods that's just fun to eat. This recipe is for a basic vanilla-and-sugar pudding, though you can add a variety of seasonings to your liking, like cinnamon, lemon, fruit, and even chocolate!

Ingredients:

1 ¼ cups almond milk
½ cup water
⅓ cup sugar
½ split vanilla bean
⅓ cup seed tapioca pearls

Cooking Tip: If you want a more porridge-like consistency, add ½ cup more of milk.

Directions:

1. Pour 1 cup of water into your Instant Pot.
2. Rinse tapioca pearls.
3. In a 4-bowl bowl (safe for pressure cooker), add tapioca, water, milk, sugar, and vanilla and mix.
4. When the sugar has dissolved, lower into steamer basket and then into cooker.
5. Select "manual," and cook on high pressure for 8 minutes.
6. When time is up, hit "cancel" and wait for the pressure to come down on its own.
7. When pressure is released, wait 5 minutes before opening the lid.
8. Stir.
9. Serve warm or cool in a fridge (covered with cling wrap) for at least

3 hours.

Nutritional Info (¼ recipe):

Total calories: 187
Protein: 2.5
Carbs: 39.6
Fiber: .1
Fat: 2.5

Buckwheat Apple Cobbler (Oil Free)

Serves: 4-6
Time: 12 minutes

Buckwheat is one of the healthiest grains out there, and is perfect for a rustic apple cobbler made right in your pressure cooker. Everything cooks together for just 12 minutes with no oil or fat. Chopped dates help add moisture and an earthy, nutty flavor that compliments sweet apples.

Ingredients:

3 pounds chopped apples
2 ½ cups water
½ cup chopped Medjool dates
½ cup dry buckwheat
2 teaspoons cinnamon
¼ teaspoon ground nutmeg
¼ teaspoon ground ginger

Directions:

1. Mix everything in your Instant Pot.
2. Click "manual," and cook for 12 minutes on high pressure.
3. When time is up, hit "cancel" and carefully quick-release.
4. Serve right away!

Nutritional Info (⅙ recipe):

Total calories: 197
Protein: 3
Carbs: 47
Fiber: 7.8
Fat: 1

Vegan Cheesecake w/ Raspberries

<u>Serves</u>: 6
<u>Time</u>: 24-38 minutes (10 minute prep time, 4-8 minute cook time, 10-20 minute natural pressure release)

Prep time is only officially 10 minutes for this creamy, rich vegan cheesecake, but you will notice that the ingredients call for soaked dates and cashews. To soak dates, submerge them in hot water for 30 minutes or so until they are very soft. For the cashews, put them in a pot and cover with water. Turn your burner on and bring the water to a rolling boil. Quickly cover with a lid and remove from heat. After 15 minutes, drain. I like fresh raspberries on my cheesecake, but you can substitute any favorite fruit.

<u>Ingredients:</u>

Crust
1 ½ cup almonds
½ cup soaked dates

Filling
1 ½ cup soaked cashews
½ cup firm silken tofu
¼ cup pure maple syrup
¼ cup unsweetened almond milk
½ lemon's worth of zest and juice
1 teaspoon pure vanilla
Pinch of salt
Fresh raspberries

<u>Directions:</u>

1. Grease six ramekins with a coconut-oil based spray.
2. To make the crust, pulse almonds until you get a crumb texture.
3. Add dates and pulse until sticky and together.

4. Press crust down into your ramekins, and up the sides a little.
5. Stick in the fridge for now.
6. To make filling, add the rest of the ingredients to a blender and pulse until smooth.
7. Divide among the ramekins and cover with foil.
8. Pour 1 ½ cups water into your pressure cooker and add trivet.
9. Set as many ramekins that fit on the trivet, and seal the lid.
10. Hit "manual" and cook for just 4 minutes.
11. When time is up, hit "cancel" and wait 10 minutes before quick-releasing.
12. Cheesecake will wobble a little, but the center should be set, like a jello.
13. Repeat with any remaining ramekins.
14. Garnish with raspberries and enjoy!

Nutritional Info (⅙ recipe per serving):

Total calories: 429
Protein: 13
Carbs: 34
Fat: 32
Fiber: 6.1

Black Rice Pudding with Coconut (Oil Free)

Serves: 6-8

Time: 1 hour, 15 minutes (5 minutes prep time, 40 minutes cook time, 20 minutes natural release, 10 minutes simmer time)

Black rice, also known as "forbidden" rice, is a lot healthier than its paler siblings. It's packed with antioxidants and iron, which is especially important for vegans. It also has more fiber and protein than white, brown, or red rice. This pudding is a delicious way to consume this superfood as it's steeped with a cheesecloth of whole spices like cinnamon, cloves, and cardamom.

Ingredients:

6 ½ cups water
2 cups black rice
¾ cup sugar
½ cup dried flaked coconut
2 cinnamon sticks, snapped in half
5 crushed cardamom pods
3 cloves
½ teaspoon salt

Directions:

1. Rinse the rice and pick out any stones.
2. Pour water into your cooker, and add rice and salt.
3. Turn on the pot to "sauté" to start heating it.
4. Add sugar and stir until it's dissolved and the bottom isn't gritty.
5. Wrap whole spices in a cheesecloth bag, tie it up, and put it in the pot.
6. Close and seal lid.
7. Hit "manual," and adjust time to 40 minutes on high pressure.
8. When time is up, let the pressure come down naturally after you hit

"cancel."
9. Open the cooker to stir the rice around.
10. Add coconut and turn your pot back to sauté until the rice liquid has become thick and syrupy.
11. When the consistency is the way you want it, take out the spice bag.
12. Serve warm or chill before eating.

Nutritional Info (⅛ recipe):

Total calories: 135
Protein: 3.4
Carbs: 26
Fiber: 2.6
Fat: 3.2

Pumpkin-Spice Brown Rice Pudding with Dates (Oil Free)

<u>Serves</u>: 6

<u>Time</u>: 1 hour, 5 minutes (10 minutes prep time, 10 minutes cook time, 10 minutes natural release, 5 minutes simmer time, 30 minutes cool time)

This isn't your grandmother's rice pudding, no offense to her. Instead of white rice, we go with brown rice, which has more nutrients like fiber and protein. To up the creaminess factor, there's pumpkin puree, and your pudding ends up tasting like pumpkin pie.

<u>Ingredients:</u>

3 cups almond milk
1 cup pumpkin puree
1 cup brown rice
1 stick cinnamon
½ cup maple syrup
½ cup water
½ cup chopped pitted dates
1 teaspoon vanilla extract
1 teaspoon pumpkin spice
⅛ teaspoon salt

<u>Directions:</u>

1. Pour boiling water over your rice and wait at least 10 minutes.
2. Rinse.
3. Pour milk and water in your Instant Pot.
4. Turn on cooker to sauté and when boiling, add rice, cinnamon, salt, and dates.
5. Close and seal lid.
6. Hit "manual" and cook on high pressure for 10 minutes.
7. Hit "cancel" when the timer goes off and wait for the pressure to

descend naturally.

8. Add pumpkin puree, maple syrup, and pumpkin spice.
9. Turn sauté back on and stir for 3-5 minutes until thick.
10. Turn off cooker.
11. Pick out cinnamon stick and add vanilla.
12. Move pudding to a bowl and cover in plastic wrap, so the plastic touches the top.
13. Wait 30 minutes to cool.
14. Serve warm or chilled.

Nutritional Info (⅙ recipe):

Total calories: 193
Protein: 1
Carbs: 38
Fiber: 4
Fat: 3

Chocolate Cheesecake

<u>Serves</u>: 6-8

<u>Time</u>: 6 hours, 10 minutes (5 minutes prep time, 55 minutes cook time, 10 minutes natural release, 5 hours chill time)

There's nothing quite like a chocolatey, creamy, cold bite of cheesecake. Like the other cheesecake recipe, this one uses cashews to get the creaminess that usually comes from dairy, as well as vegan chocolate chips and chocolate almond milk. The crust is a simple mixture of almond flour, sugar, and coconut oil. You can also buy vegan-friendly crust if you like.

<u>Ingredients:</u>

1 ½ cups almond flour
½ cup sugar
¼ cup melted coconut oil

1 ½ cups soaked and drained cashews
1 cup chocolate almond milk
⅔ cup sugar
¼ cup vegan chocolate chips
2 tablespoons coconut flour
2 teaspoons vanilla
½ teaspoon salt

<u>Directions:</u>

1. Mix the ingredients in the first list together.
2. Press crust into the bottom of a 7-inch springform pan and 1-inch up the sides.
3. Put in fridge while you make the filling.
4. Mix the second ingredient list together (minus chocolate chips and flour) in a food processor until smooth.

5. Add coconut flour and mix.
6. Add chocolate chips and mix with a spatula until evenly-incorporated.
7. Pour batter in crust.
8. Pour 1 1/3 cups of water into your cooker and lower in the steamer basket or trivet.
9. Put pan into cooker and close and seal the lid.
10. Select "manual" and cook on high pressure for 55 minutes.
11. When time is up, hit "cancel" and wait 10 minutes before quick-releasing pressure.
12. Carefully remove the pan and cool for 1 hour.
13. Cover the cheesecake and freeze for 4 hours, before moving to fridge or serving.

Nutritional Info (⅛ recipe):

Total calories: 493
Protein: 10
Carbs: 42
Fiber: 1
Fat: 29

Pineapple Upside-Down Cake

Serves: 6

Time: 1 hour, 22 minutes (10 minute prep time, 22 minute cook time, 10 minute natural pressure release, 40 minute cool time)

This cake classic doesn't have a ton of ingredients, so it comes together with just 10 minutes of prep time. The rest of the time is just spent waiting for the cake to cook in the Instant Pot, and then cooling so the cake inverts perfectly, revealing the golden pineapple rings and bits of strawberry.

Ingredients:

1 ⅓ cups whole-wheat flour
4 pineapple rings
⅓ cup rapeseed oil
⅓ cup unsweetened almond milk
¾ cup + ¼ cup white sugar
3 ½ tablespoons vegan butter
1 teaspoon pure vanilla
1 teaspoon apple cider vinegar
½ teaspoon baking powder
¾ teaspoon baking soda
¼ teaspoon salt
Pieces of fresh strawberry

Directions:

1. Mix ¼ cup of sugar and butter together.
2. Spread on the bottom of your cooker-safe cake dish, and up the sides, too.
3. Lay down pineapple slices in the dish.
4. Add in some pieces of strawberry.
5. In a bowl, mix flour, baking soda, baking powder, and salt.
6. Mix milk and apple cider vinegar together.

7. Into that mixture, add rapeseed oil, vanilla, and the rest of the sugar.
8. Mix wet into dry until just combined.
9. Pour the batter into your dish and cover with foil.
10. Pour 1 cup of water into your pressure cooker and lower in trivet.
11. Set dish on trivet, and seal the lid.
12. Cook on "manual" for 22 minutes on high pressure.
13. When time is up, hit "cancel" and wait about 10 minutes for a natural pressure release.
14. Remove any excess pressure.
15. Unwrap the dish and let it cool for 30 minutes before inverting.
16. Cool another 10 minutes before slicing!

Nutritional Info (⅙ recipe per serving):

Total calories: 342
Protein: 4
Carbs: 44
Fat: 18
Fiber: 2.8

Orange-Glazed Poached Pears

<u>Serves</u>: 4

<u>Time</u>: 17 minutes (5 minutes prep time, 12 minutes cook time)

Pears are one of the best dessert fruits. They have a sweet, but not cloying flavor, and they absorb spices exceptionally well. For this recipe, you poach fresh pears in the pressure cooker, while at the same time, the pot prepares a spiced orange glaze. The dessert looks fancy, but it involves almost no work.

<u>Ingredients:</u>

4 ripe pears
1 cup orange juice
⅓ cup sugar
1 cinnamon stick
2 teaspoons cinnamon
1 teaspoon nutmeg
1 teaspoon ginger
1 teaspoon ground clove

<u>Directions:</u>

1. Peel the pears, leaving the stem alone.
2. Pour 1 cup of orange juice into your cooker and add spices.
3. Arrange pears in the steamer basket and lower in the cooker.
4. Close and seal the lid.
5. Click "manual" and adjust time to 7 minutes on high pressure.
6. When time is up, press "cancel" and wait 5 minutes before quick-releasing.
7. Carefully remove trivet and pears.
8. Pick out the cinnamon stick.
9. Turn your pot to sauté and add sugar.
10. Stir until the liquid has reduced to a sauce.

11. Serve pears with sauce poured on top.

Nutritional Info (¼ recipe):

Total calories: 188
Protein: 1
Carbs: 49
Fiber: 6
Fat: 0

Stuffed Pears with Salted Caramel Sauce

Serves: 4

Time: 39 minutes (10 minutes prep time, 9 minutes cook time, 10 minutes natural release, 10 minutes reduction time)

We've glazed pears in this book, so now how about we stuff them? It's amazing how good some oats, vegan butter, sugar, nuts, and raisins are together. And when you put that inside a fresh, sweet pear? And *then* you drizzle the whole thing in a homemade pressure-cooker caramel? You'll be dreaming about this dessert when pears are in season.

Ingredients:

2 ripe, firm pears
½ cup water + 2 tablespoons
¼ cup raisins
¼ rolled oats
¼ cup walnuts
¼ cup sugar
3 tablespoons vegan butter
1 teaspoon vanilla extract
½ teaspoon cinnamon
¼ teaspoon sea salt

Directions:

1. Cut pears in half and spoon out a well in the center.
2. Mix 1 tablespoon of butter with oats, raisins, walnuts, vanilla, and cinnamon in your food processor.
3. When mixture is like a crumble, stuff the pears.
4. Pour 2 tablespoons of water and sugar in your Instant Pot.
5. Turn on to "sauté" and cook until the water has become dark amber.
6. Pour in the rest of the water.

7. Pour pears in the cooker.
8. Click "manual" and adjust to 9 minutes on low pressure.
9. When time is up, hit "cancel" and wait 10 minutes before quick-releasing.
10. Turn the pot back to "sauté" after removing the pears and reduce for 10 minutes.
11. Whisk in 2 tablespoons of butter and ¼ teaspoon salt.
12. Serve pears with caramel sauce on top.

Nutritional Info (¼ recipe):

Total calories: 244
Protein: 2
Carbs: 35
Fiber: 3.75
Fat: 12

Cinnamon-Poached Pears with Chocolate Sauce

<u>Serves</u>: 6

<u>Time</u>: 10 minutes (5 minutes prep time, 3 minutes cook time, 2 minutes stovetop)

So far, none of the pear desserts have involved chocolate. Let's change that. After poaching pears in a syrup infused with cinnamon, you melt a chocolate sauce made from coconut oil and coconut milk, and pour it over your pears. It's decadent and quick.

<u>Ingredients:</u>

6 ripe, firm pears
6 cinnamon sticks
3 cups water
2 cups sugar
2 cups white wine
1 halved lemon

9-ounces chopped bittersweet chocolate
½ cup coconut milk
¼ cup coconut oil
2 tablespoons maple syrup

<u>Directions:</u>

1. Pour water, wine, sugar, and cinnamon into your Instant Pot.
2. Hit "sauté" and stir until the sugar dissolves.
3. Turn the cooker to "keep warm."
4. Peel pears, keeping the stems.
5. Rub with the cut lemon.
6. Squeeze juice into the cooker and drop in lemon.
7. Put pears in the pot.

8. Close and seal lid.
9. Hit "manual," and cook for 3 minutes on high pressure.
10. Press "cancel" and then quick-release pressure.
11. Take out the pears and let them cool before pouring on pressure cooker syrup.
12. For chocolate sauce, put chocolate in a bowl.
13. Heat coconut oil, coconut milk, and syrup in a saucepan until it just begins to boil.
14. Pour over chocolate and stir until smooth.
15. Pour over the pears.

Nutritional Info (⅙ recipe):

Total calories: 210
Protein: 2.8
Carbs: 50
Fiber: 7.5
Fat: 1.6

Apricot-Pear Cake (Oil Free)

<u>Serves:</u> 4-6
<u>Time:</u> 55 minutes (5 minutes prep time, 35 minutes cook time, 15 minutes natural release)

This simple, steamed cake is moist and studded with fresh pears and dried apricots. You can add any fruit you would like, depending on what's in season, so consider this a go-to cake for whenever you need to bring something to a bake sale or to a gathering.

<u>Ingredients:</u>

1 ½ cups water
1 cup fresh chopped pears
½ cup dried apricots

1 ¼ cups whole-wheat flour
½ teaspoon baking soda
½ teaspoon baking powder
½ teaspoon ground nutmeg
⅛ teaspoon salt

½ cup unsweetened coconut milk
¼ cup pure maple syrup
2 tablespoons organic applesauce
2 tablespoons ground golden flax seeds

<u>Directions:</u>

1. Grease a 7-inch Bundt pan.
2. Mix dry ingredients in a bowl.
3. Mix wet ingredients in a separate bowl.
4. Mix wet into dry before folding in pears and cranberries.
5. Pour batter into pan and wrap in foil.

6. Pour water into your pressure cooker and lower in trivet or steamer basket.
7. Lower the pan in.
8. Close and seal lid.
9. Select "manual" and cook on high pressure for 35 minutes.
10. When time is up, hit "cancel" and let the pressure come down on its own.
11. Take out the pan and throw away the foil.
12. Cool before serving.

Nutritional Info (⅙ recipe):
Total calories: 163
Protein: 4
Carbs: 35
Fiber: 2
Fat: 2

Chocolate Fondue w/ Coconut Cream

Serves: 2-4
Time: Under 5 minutes

Chocolate fondue, liquid chocolate, might be the perfect dessert for chocoholics. To veganize, you use coconut cream instead of dairy dream. Serve with a big platter of cookies, fresh fruit, marshmallows, and anything else you think might be good dipped in chocolate.

Ingredients:

2 cups water
3.5-ounces 70% dark bittersweet chocolate
3.5-ounces coconut cream
1 teaspoon sugar

Directions:

1. Pour 2 cups of water into your Instant Pot and lower in trivet.
2. In a heatproof bowl, add chocolate chunks.
3. Add coconut cream and sugar.
4. Put the bowl on top of the trivet.
5. Close and seal the lid.
6. Hit "manual" and cook on high pressure for 2 minutes.
7. When time is up, hit "cancel" and quick-release.
8. Carefully remove bowl and whisk with a fork until it becomes smooth.
9. Serve!

Nutritional Info (¼ recipe):

Total calories: 216
Protein: 1.8
Carbs: 11.7
Fiber: 2.6
Fat: 20.3

Conclusion

I hope that this book has inspired you to try out more vegan recipes, even if you aren't a vegan or are still in the transitional phase where you're adding food, and not eliminating just yet. Being a vegan does not mean sacrificing quality or diversity when it comes to food, so don't let anyone discourage you with comments about how you're "missing out."

A pressure cooker, in particular the Instant Pot, is the must-have tool for vegans. This book covered how to use the Instant Pot, how to keep it clean and well-maintained, and provided cooking charts on the most common ingredients you'll be using as a vegan. Whether you're making beans, lentils, pasta, oats, veggies, or fruit, the Instant Pot is significantly faster than any other cooking method, and preserves the most nutrition. It's a double-win.

Your health should be a top priority. When you're in good health, everything else is easier. Vegan food prepared with a pressure cooker is the single best way to improve your health without complicating your life. Please come back to this book and its awesome recipes again and again to continue your vegan journey. I love walking alongside you.

Index: Converting slow cooker recipes to pressure cookers

If you're reading this book, you're probably a person who has used slow cookers in the past, because you want to make cooking convenient. That means you have lots of slow cooker recipes, and you don't want them to go to waste now that you're using an Instant Pot. You can usually find pressure cooker versions of just about any slow cooker recipe, but in case you can't, you can convert those recipes to a pressure cooker. Here's how:

Step 1: The aromatics

Aromatics are the first ingredients you cook. They add flavor and depth to the dish. Aromatics include herbs, whole spices, celery, garlic, carrots, and onions. Look and see what aromatics the slow cooker recipe uses, and cook those right at the beginning before following the rest of the recipe.

Step 2: The liquid

Pressure cookers need much less liquid than slow cookers. They basically end with the amount of liquid that you started with. Find out how much liquid the slow cooker recipe ends with, and put that in your Instant Pot, plus ½ cup.

Step 3: The cooking time

An easy rule for converting to pressure cooker time is to reduce the time given in the slow cooker recipe by ⅔. It's always better to go with a lower time, because you can always cook underdone food more, while overcooked food can't be fixed.

Step 4: The amount of food

The last step is to see how full the slow cooker is. If following the slow cooker recipe would result in your Instant Pot being more than ⅔ of the way full (½ for pastas, rice, oatmeal, beans), you'll need to cut the recipe down or cook in separate batches.

Thank you so much for reading this book!

I hope the book was able to teach you how pressure cooking can simplify your everyday life.

Finally, if you enjoyed this book, then I'd like to ask you for a favor, would you be kind enough to leave a review for this book on Amazon? It'd be greatly appreciated!

Preview of Instant Pot Cookbook: A Complete Instant Pot Pressure Cooker Cookbook with 115 Fast, Easy, and Irresistible Recipes for Amazingly Tasty, and Healthy Meals

Good home cooking is a lost art. Yes, it seems that everywhere you look there are food blogs and celebrity chefs presenting beautiful meals and recipes, but the average person just doesn't have the time or skills or energy to pull most of them off. That's really sad, because cooking at home can be really fun, and also extremely healthy and cost-effective. Luckily, there's a way to enjoy all the benefits of home cooking without spending a lot of time slaving away in the kitchen.

The answer: pressure cooking. It's a cooking method that's been around for a long time, but until recent decades, it wasn't that easy, and even a little dangerous. Now, there are electric pressure cookers, which combine the ease of slow cookers and speed of a microwave. The Instant Pot in particular is a fantastic pressure cooker. If you're a person who gets nervous in the kitchen and easily intimidated by all the tools that you see on the Food Network, the Instant Pot can become your go-to resource for fast, healthy recipes.

This book will walk you through every aspect of owning an Instant Pot, from understanding what the buttons mean, to cooking with it, to cleaning it. The bulk of the book consists of all the kinds of dishes you can make with the cooker, including breakfast, quick weekday meals, holiday dinners and sides, and awesome desserts. Even if you rarely set foot in the kitchen before, you'll find yourself excited to try out the recipes, and eager to share what you've learned with friends and family. Let's get started!

I would love to give you a gift. Please visit happyhealthycookingonline.com to get these 4 amazing eBooks for free!

MY OTHER BOOKS

Instant Pot Cookbook: A Comprehensive Instant Pot Pressure Cooker Cookbook with 110 Amazing Recipes for Healthy, Fast, and Delicious Meals

Instant Pot Cookbook: A Complete Instant Pot Pressure Cooker Cookbook with 115 Fast, Easy, and Irresistible Recipes for Amazingly Tasty, and Healthy Meals

Instant Pot Cookbook: A Comprehensive Instant Pot Pressure Cooker Cookbook with 200 Quick, Easy, and Healthy Recipes for Amazingly Delicious Meals

Instant Pot Cookbook: An Extensive Instant Pot Pressure Cooker Cookbook with 225 Fast, Easy, and Healthy Recipes for Incredibly Delicious and Nourishing Meals

Instant Pot Cookbook: 5 Ingredients or Less - 100 Quick, Easy, and Amazingly Tasty Instant Pot Recipes for Healthy and Delicious Pressure Cooker Meals

Power Pressure Cooker XL Cookbook: 150 Amazing Electric Pressure Cooker Recipes for Fast, Healthy, and Incredibly Tasty Meals

Power Pressure Cooker XL Cookbook: 200 Irresistible Electric Pressure Cooker Recipes for Fast, Healthy, and Amazingly Delicious Meals

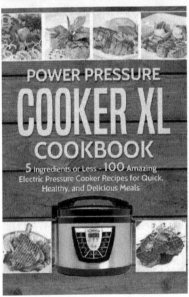

Power Pressure Cooker XL Cookbook: 5 Ingredients or Less - 100 Amazing Electric Pressure Cooker Recipes for Quick, Healthy, and Delicious Meals

Made in the USA
Middletown, DE
13 July 2017